Virginia County Records

VOLUME III

WILLIAMSBURG WILLS

Being Transcriptions from the Original Files
at the Chancery Court of Williamsburg

EDITED BY

William Armstrong Crozier

CLEARFIELD

Originally Published As
Virginia County Records
Volume III
The Genealogical Association
New York, 1906

Reprinted
Southern Book Company
Baltimore, 1954

Reissued
Genealogical Publishing Company, Inc.
Baltimore, 1973

Reprinted for
Clearfield Company, Inc. by
Genealogical Publishing Co., Inc.
Baltimore, Maryland
1995

Library of Congress Catalogue Card Number 67-29835
International Standard Book Number 0-8063-0567-3

Virginia County Records

Williamsburg Wills

BEING TRANSCRIPTIONS FROM THE ORIGINAL FILES AT
THE CHANCERY COURT OF WILLIAMSBURG

EDITED BY

William Armstrong Crozier, F. R. S.

*Editor of Records of Spotsylvania County ; Virginia Colonial
Militia; The Buckners of Virginia; Crozier's
American Armory, Etc., Etc.*

VOL. III.

PUBLISHED BY

THE GENEALOGICAL ASSOCIATION

NEW YORK   MDCCCCVI

Introductory

AMES CITY COUNTY was one of the eight original shires into which the Colony of Virginia was divided in 1634. Williamsburg, the present county seat, was at a very early period, the seat of a District Court. It was the capital of the State from the year 1699 until 1779, when the public records were removed to Richmond, which henceforth became the capital of Virginia.

During the Civil War, the court records were removed to Richmond for protection against the vandalism of the Federal troops. This protection was but a temporary one, for the records were almost entirely destroyed in the great fire in Richmond at the evacuation in 1865.

Williamsburg being a Chancery Court, it followed that depositions, court orders, and copies of wills in numerous suits from various counties were deposited there; and it is with the few records that were saved from destruction that this volume treats.

In the present work there will be found abstracts of all wills now on file at the Chancery Court. In a large number of instances, the original records of the counties from which these wills were taken, have been destroyed, and the copies at Williamsburg are the only ones in existence. It is unnecessary, therefore, to enlarge upon their great value to the antiquary and genealogist.

Upon examining the records, it was found that all wills coming under the initial letter A, and a portion under the letter B, were missing. Fortunately, an alphabetical list of the wills had been made by Dr. Lyon G. Tyler, President of

William and Mary College, and Prof. E. J. Stubbs of the same institution. Through the courtesy of the latter gentleman, I have been able to make use of this list, thereby supplying the name of the testator, and the dates of the missing wills.

I feel assured that the loss of these records—fortunately only a small number—is but a temporary one, and that they will eventually be recovered. When this is accomplished, they will be printed and sent gratis to all the subscribers to this volume.

WILLIAM ARMSTRONG CROZIER.

Williamsburg Wills

ARMISTEAD, ROBERT, York Co., — Feb., 173—; codicil 19 March, 1741-2; pro. Elizabeth City, 19 May, 1742.

ADAMS, ROBERT, Fairfax Co., 25 Feb., 1789; 16 June, 1789.

ADAMS, HENRY, Southampton Co., 7 Jan., 1800; 19 Feb., 1800.

ATKINSON, JAMES, Isle of Wight Co., 8 May, 1816; 5 March, 1819.

ARCHER, EDWARD, Norfolk Borough, 13 Nov., 1771; — Dec., 1771.

ANDREWS, ROBERT, City of Williamsburg, 17 July, 1803. No date probate.

ALLEN, RICHMOND, New Kent Co., — July, 1807; 14 April, 1808.

ALLEN, WILLIAM, New Kent Co., — July 1807; 14 April, 1808.

ANDERSON, JOHN, Mathews Co., 27 July, 1808. No date probate.

ARMISTEAD, ELIZABETH, Mathews Co., — July, 1814; 30 May, 1815.

BOHANNON, AMBROSE, Essex Co., 8 Jan. 1753; 22 Feb., 1753.

BINNS, THOMAS, New Kent Co., 4 June, 1799; 10 April, 1800.

BENN, CHRISTIAN, Nansemond Co., 30 March, 1799; 8 April, 1799.

BEARD, RICHARD, Norfolk Borough, 7 May, 1817; 25 Aug., 1817.

BERRYMAN, JOHN, Lancaster Co., 16 Feb., 1786; codicil 31 March, 1786; 18 April, 1787.

WILLIAMSBURG WILLS

BAKER, ELIZABETH, Nansemond Co., 20 Aug., 1798; 14 April, 1801.

BILLUPS, RICHARD, Gloucester Co., 31 Jan., 1751; 27 Feb., 1752.

BAILEY, JAMES, Westmoreland Co., 1 Feb., 1780; 29 Apl., 1784.

BAILEY, DANIEL, Westmoreland Co., 17 Oct., 1785; 30 Nov., 1786.

BANISTER, JOHN, Dinwiddie Co., 9 Jan., 1788; 20 Oct., 1788.

BOOTH, THOMAS, Hanover Co., 16 Feb., 1753; 2 Sept., 1756.

BOSWELL, MACHEN, Mathews Co., 21 April, 1793; 13 Jan., 1794.

BREWER, JOHN, Nansemond Co., 15 March, 1814; 9 May, 1814. Son John; dau. Nancy Rogers, plantation purchased from William Cowper; dau. Sally Rogers; dau. Polly Brewer; grandson America Rogers; my sister Eliz. Vardeman. Exrs. son John and son-in-law Thomas Rogers. Wit. Jeremiah Brewer, Elizabeth Vardeman, Josiah Brewer.

BRACK, RICHARD, James City Co., 9 Feb., 1789; 13 Apl., 1789. Wife Mary; children Martha, William, Mary, Burwell, Jack, Elizabeth and Eleanor Brack; friends Edmund Cowles and Wm. Lightfoot. Exrs. wife Mary and son Burwell, also to be guardian to dau. Elizabeth. Wit. Henry Cowles, Elizabeth Henly, Robert Walker, John Cooper.

BUCKNER, BALDWIN MATHEWS, Ware Parish, Gloucester Co., 5 April, 1774; 5 Nov., 1778. To my younger sons a tract of land as they shall come of age; son Thomas Buckner; son Samuel Buckner; exrs. to pay twenty-five shillings annually to Sarah Lemmon. Exrs. brother John Buckner, brother Mordecai Buckner, friends John Cary and John Chisman and my sons Thomas, Samuel, Robert and

6

WILLIAMSBURG WILLS

John Buckner. Wit. John Elliot, John Tompkins, George Booth, Jr., John Buckner.

BUNTING, WILLIAM, Norfolk Co., 23 May, 1801; 22 Dec., 1801. Daughters-in-law Abigail and Jannet Owens; dau. Polly Bunting. Exrs. Edward Herbert and John Moore. Wit. John Moore, Nathl. Dyes, Benj. Bunting.

BOYD, SPENCER, King and Queen Co., 7 Dec., 1778; 10 May, 1779. Wife Lucy and mentions articles of agreement made with her dated 20 Aug., 1766, before their marriage; son James; sons Robert, Spencer and William; dau. Julia; nephew Spencer Boyd and his sister Elizabeth; the child my wife now goes with. Exrs. William and Henry Todd of King and Queen Co. Wit. John Gardner, Anthony Gardner, Isaac Digges, Thomas Brown.

BUTT, ARTHUR Norfolk Co., (nuncupative), 20 March, 1821; 10 Apl., 1822. My nephews Robert B. Butt, John N. Butt and Horatio E. Hall to have equal division of the estate and to be exrs. My sister Frances Butt to have $150 dollars per year for life. Presented and proved by the oaths of Richard Baugh and Edward D. Wilson.

BURT, PHILIP, York Co., 9 July, 1793; 22 May, 1798. Wife Anna; son Thomas Burt and Nathl. Burwell to be exrs. Wit. Carter Burwell, Edward Brooks, Philip Dedman, Snr.

BRIDGER, MARTHA, widow and relict of John Bridger, Isle of Wight Co., 15 Jan., 1789; 5 Feb., 1789. William, son of Mallory Todd; to Mrs. Martha Vanwagener; to Fanny Robinson Todd; godson Joseph Hodsden; to Mrs. Keziah Harvey, Miss Frances Day, Miss Eliz. Day, Miss Sarah Diggs, Miss Polly Diggs; my son Joseph Bridger; my sisters Mrs. Mary Davis, Mrs. Frances Brown and Mrs. Keziah Harvey; the children of my sister Angelina Todd and my brother William Mallory. Exrs. brother-in-law Capt. Mallory Todd, and my brother William Mallory. Wit. Richard Todd, John Day, Tabitha Wrenn.

7

BRIDGER, JOSEPH, Smithfield, Isle of Wight Co., 7 Jan. 1795; 6 Apl., 1795. My guardian Mallory Todd; Mary Diggs of Smithfield; cousin Wm. Harvey; cousin Joseph Hodsden; Mallory Moore Todd; Fanny Todd dau. of Mallory Todd; Aunt Esther Bridger. Exr. Mallory Todd, Snr., of Smithfield. Wit. Merit M. Robinson, John Casey, William Garton.

BRUCE, WM. MOORE, Norfolk Co., 11 May, 1792; 17 Feb., 1794. Son Joseph; mentions land of Edward and Archibald Bruce; dau. Catherine Batts Bruce; dau. Mary Batts Bruce. Exrs. brother Archibald Bruce and John Shield. Wit. William Rhonnalds, Henry Lowe, William Carney.

BRANCH, POLLY, Southampton Co., 24 Jan., 1814; 19 Dec., 1814. Sisters Elizabeth and Sally Branch; brother Benj. Branch. Exr. Capt. James Clayton. Wit. Goodman Branch, Eliza Stephenson, Bennett Stephenson.

BRANCH, ELIZABETH, Isle of Wight Co., 13 June, 1816; 5 Aug., 1816. Sister Sally Jefferson; brother-in-law Samuel Jefferson; Patsy wife of my brother Burwell Branch; nephew Charles, son of Francis Branch; niece Emma Branch, dau. of Burwell Branch; niece Martha Branch, dau. of Burwell Branch. Exr. brother-in-law Saml. Jefferson. Wit. Jordan Parr, Francis Chapman.

BOUSH, GOODRICH (nuncupative), Borough of Norfolk, but now living in James City, 17 Aug., 1778; 19 Dec., 1782. Wife Mary; sons William, Samuel and James; daughters Ann, Mary and Elizabeth Boush. Exrs. wife Mary, brothers Samuel and Arthur Boush and friends James Holt and Malachi Wilson.

BOHANNON, AMBROSE, Parish So. Farnham, Essex Co., 24 Feb., 1776; 15 Dec., 1800. Entire estate to brother Joseph Bohannon. Wit. Thomas Miller, William Miller, Dorothy Miller.

WILLIAMSBURG WILLS

BOUSH, JOHN, Borough of Norfolk, and Clerk of Co. Court of Norfolk; 24 July, 1790; 28 May, 1792. Wife Frances Moseley Boush, and the child she now goes with; to brother Robert Boush and my two sisters. Exrs. wife and James Nimmo. Wit. Samuel Shepherd, Willis Whitfield.

BOYD, DAVID, Gent., Par. of St. Stephen's, Northumberland Co., 7 May, 1781; 10 Dec., 1781. Mentions estate of late Mr. John Yerby; my late dau. Margaret Smith; Augustine Jaquilin Smith son of my said dau.; to David McCullock son of John McCullock of Torhouse and Mary his wife, my youngest sister, of the Shire of Wigton in North Britain; James McCullock son of John McCullock and Agnes his wife late of the Isle of Man; granddau. Mary Jacqulin Smith; my estate in North Britain to sister Mary McCullock; I desire my aforesaid grandson to carry my bones and those of his mother and his uncle Alexander Boyd to Scotland, and have them buried by the side of my father and mother in the churchyard of the town of Wigton; wife Margaret Boyd, Col. John Smith of Frederick Co. and Rev. Thomas Smith of Westmoreland Co. guardians to my grandchildren, and also exrs. together with Richard Mitchell of Lancaster Co., Capt. David Ball and Mr. Onesiphorous Harney of Northumberland Co., Mr. John Sydnor, Capt. Williamson Ball, Mr. Wm. Miskell and Major Charles McCarty of Richmond Co., and William Taylor, Gent., of Northumberland Co. No wit.

BROOKE, WILLIAM, King and Queen Co., 4 Feb., 1804; 18 Sept., 1804. Brother Richard Brooke; sister Catherine Tunstall; the three children of my decd. sister Mary Hill; nephew Thomas Daniel Price and my nieces the two unmarried daus. of Robert Price. Exr. brother Richard Brooke. Wit. Henry Young, Charles Smith, George M. Brooke.

BOYKIN, FRANCIS, SNR., Isle of Wight Co., 7 Oct., 1803; 2 April, 1805. Daughter Nancy Boykin; sons John and

9

Francis M. Boykin; Benj. Stringfield, Jnr. Exrs. son Francis and Andrew Woodby. Wit. William Chapman, Daniel Whitby, Samuel Brany.

BOUSHELL, WILLIAM, SNR., District of St. Brides, Norfolk Co., 18 Sept., 1793; 28 Jan., 1795. My wife; daus. Betsy and Nancy Frances; son Thomas. Exrs. sons James and William. Wit. Christopher Bromadges, Christopher Gardner, Richd. Webb.

BURWELL, ROBERT, Isle of Wight Co., 16 Aug., 1772; 13 Oct. 1777. To only son Nathaniel Burwell; son-in-law John Page, Esq., of Rosewell; my dau. Frances Page; to dau. Burwell wife of son Nathaniel. Exrs. son Nathaniel, son-in-law John Page, Robert C. Nicholas, the Honl. William Nelson and my cousin Thomas Nelson, Esq. Wit. John Jones, Catherine Mathews. Codicil, 10 Jan., 1777, wherein testator is now of King and Queen Co., states that he has now married Mary Braxton. Wit. W. Ellzey, Saml. Baker, Thomas Bragg. 2d codicil, 10 Jan., 1777, mentions grandson Robert Carter Burwell; cousin Thomas Nelson; son-in-law John Page.

BRADLEY, JAMES, Par. of Westover, Charles City Co., 17 Aug., 1803; 15 Sept., 1803. Daughter Betty C. Bradley; Robert Jackson; grandsons Robert and Mitchal Bradley and their mother Susannah; sister Mourning Bradley. Exrs. grandson Robert and friend William Clopton. Wit. William Lyon, Littleton Bradley.

BRADENHAM, JOHN, Par. of Blisland, New Kent Co., 30 Aug., 1795; 8 Oct., 1795. Wife Mary; son Robert; daus. Elizabeth Hockaday, Susanna Harman and Sally Sale; grandson John Sandford Allen; son-in-law James Chandler; grandson Robert Bradenham Chandler. Exrs. son Robert and son-in-law William Hockaday. Wit. William Parrish, James Williams, Edward Jones.

WILLIAMSBURG WILLS

BROWNE, BENJAMIN, Surry Co., 21 April, 1819; 24 May, 1819. Daughter Lucy Power; son William H. Browne. Exrs. Charles H. Graves. Wit. Burwell Barham, Patsy Graves.

BROWNE, WILLIAM, Surry Co., (no date), 25 Jan., 1786. Son William Taylor Browne; dau. Ann Browne; my bro. Benj. E. Browne; my loving wife. Exrs. Henry Browne, Benj. E. Browne, William Browne, Jnr. No wit.

BROWN, WILLIAM, James City Co., 22 Oct., 1773; 14 Oct., 1776. Daughter Susan Christian; dau. Alice Pierce; granddaughters Ann Pierce, Alice Pierce, Alice Henley and Martha Henley; son John Brown; dau. Elizabeth Henley; son William Brown; son-in-law John Pierce; dau. Mary Brown; granddaughter Letitia Power; to John Paul; wife Alice Brown; grandsons Richardson Henley. John Pierce and Eaton Christian. Exrs. son John Brown and sons-in-law Richardson Henley and John Pierce. Wit. William Richardson, Jeremiah Martin, Sarah Cowles.

BROWNE, WILLIAM, James City Co., 31 Jan., 1808; 12 April, 1808. To the four children of my first wife, viz.: John, William, Dabney and Otway Browne; to the children of my last wife. Exrs sons John and William Browne. Wit. Thomas Harwood, William D. Waddill.

BROWNE, JOHN, James City Co., 16 Oct., 1793; 13 Jan., 1794. Daughters Susannah and Eliza; child my wife now goes with; mentions his four daughters and his son Robert Cobbs and son John Eaton. Wit. Archer Hawkins, John Hawkins, Edward Power, Jnr.

BRANCH, HENRY, Southampton Co., 5 March, 1808; 15 Aug., 1808. Sons Benjamin, Burwell, Francis, Edward and George Branch; my wife; daus. Sally and Elizabeth. Exrs. son Francis and James Clayton. Wit. James Clayton, John Vasser, Robert Adams.

WILLIAMSBURG WILLS

CHURCHILL, SALLY (nuncupative), 11 Oct., 1799. To
Miss Hannah Robinson; to mother Mrs. Elizabeth Churchill;
brother Thomas Churchill; half sister Mrs. Hannah Robinson; niece Eliz. Churchill Darby and her mother Lucy Darby
and John Darby her father. Wit. Elizabeth Berkeley. At-
tested to by Thomas Jameson 16 Oct., 1799.

NOTE : There is no name of county given in the probate of this
will, but the name of the recording clerk is O. Cosby. As Mr.
Cosby was clerk of Middlesex county from 1799 to 1806, succeeding
William Churchill who was clerk from 1772 to 1799, it is evident
that the place of probate was the above named county.

CHRISTIAN, MICHAEL, Northampton Co., 29 Nov.,
1783; 9 Dec., 1783. Daughter Margaret and her husband
William Jenne; dau. Anne Hays; dau. Susannah and her
husband Ellison Armistead; dau. Esther and her husband
John Darby; dau. Rose. Exrs. sons-in-law John Darby
Smith Snead. Wit. John Burton, John Ewing, Nicholas
Cammel.

CHRISTIAN, JOHN, New Kent Co., 14 July, 1801; 10
Sept., 1801. Son Collier Christian; son John H. Christian;
son George Christian; to Lyddall Apperson who intermarried
with my dau.; son Archibald Christian. Exr. son John.
Wit. Jones R. Christian, Richard Poindexter.

CHRISTIAN MATTHIAS, Par. of Elizabeth River, Nor-
folk Co., 30 Aug., 1788; 22 July, 1794. Stepdaughter Molly
Baynes and her husband John; stepdaughter Nancy Ashby;
dau. Lydia and her husband John Bramble. Exrs. Nancy
Ashby, John Baynes and John Bramble. Wit. John Johnson,
James Jackson, Matthew Godfrey.

CHERRY, PRISCILLA, Norfolk Co., 24 Oct., 1816; no
date of probate. All estate to Uncle John Cherry, and he
to be extr. Wit. Matthew Manning, John Moore, Alice
Cherry.

CHARLES, KEMP, Warwick Co., 20 Oct., 1781; 9 May,
1782. Wife Martha; children Thomas, Kemp, Edward, Wil-

liam, Henry, Martha, Margaret, Mary and Diana. Exrs. friends Hudson Allen and Edward Harwood. Wit. William Harwood, Thomas Lucas, John Wynne.

CARY, THOMAS W., Warwick Co., 30 Sept., 1817; 12 Aug., 1819. My dear mother not to be sent to Williamsburg; my wife and son; my wife's sister Ann Middleton. Exr. John W. Massenburg. No wit.

CALVERT, THOMAS, Princess Anne Co., 14 April, 1808; 1 March, 1813. Daughter Polly Calvert; wife Kezia; sister Polly wife of Col. Briton Jones of Southampton Co.; sister Eliza Calvert. Wit. A. Boyd, George McIntosh.

CALVERT, MAXIMILIAN, Borough of Norfolk, 18 Feb., 1781; Jan'y Court, 1782. Son Jonathan; mentions land purchased of Dr. Westwood of Liverpool; dau. Peggy Calvert; son John Savage Calvert; grandsons Maximilian Maxwell and John Greenwood Masden; daus. Mary Masden and Helen Maxwell. Exrs. wife, son Jonathan and sons-in-law James Masden and James Maxwell. Wit. Bassett Moseley, Cornelius Calvert, Charles Bushnell, Sarah Smith.

CAMPBELL, JAMES, Essex Co., 27 Feb., 1774; 20 June, 1774. Wife Sarah; son Thacher; wife's daughters Mary and Eliz. Hill. Exrs. wife and William Young. Wit. Lilian Webb, Eliz. Young, Mary Hill, Eliz. Hill, Sarah Ware.

CAMPBELL, DONALD, Borough of Norfolk, 6 Jan., 1795; 23 Feb., 1795. To Rebecca Hammers; sons Alexander and John Ormargh Campbell; Henry eldest son of my friend St. George Tucker; nephew John Gilchrist; sister Frances Hinson and her three children Frances, Elizabeth and John Gilchrist; if two sons die before the age of 21 then nephew John Gilchrist to inherit and take the name of Campbell. Exrs. St. George Tucker and John Gilchrist. Wit. John Newizon, James Taylor, Thomas Matthews, Wm. Lindsay. Codicil, dated 2 Feb., 1795, in which testator declares his friend

Rebecca Hammers to be treated as his true and lawful wife by his exrs.

CARY, THOMAS, Warwick Co., 26 Jan., 1790; 13 Dec., 1792. Wife Frances; son-in-law Edmund Custis; son William; Thomas Lucas to be guardian; Lucy Serveant and Eliz. Read Lucas; dau. Martha Lucas; son Miles; mentions lands of Richard Cary. Exrs. sons William and Miles and son-in-law Edmund Custis. Wit. William Whitaker, Moses Walrond, Carter Crafford.

CARY, ELIZABETH, Par. and Co. of Warwick, 30 Nov., 1805; 12 Dec., 1805. To be buried in family lot at Pear Tree Hall; sister Ann Cary; sister Rebecca Cary's estate; mentions her father's estate; sister Ann Wynne; nephews Richard and Miles children of my brother Richard Cary; nephew Miles son of my bro. Miles. Exrs. brothers-in-law William Dudley and William Wynne. Wit. Mary Robinson, W. W. Lee.

CAMP, REBECCA, James City, 26 Feb., 1797; 13 June, 1797. To William Keen; to Susanna Pigott all my right to estate of Thaddy Kelly decd.; John James; John Camp; William Camp; Edward son of Edward Richardson; George son of John Camp. Exrs. William Keen and John Camp. Wit. William James, Royall R. Allen, Humphrey Garrott, Jnr·

CAMPBELL, SARAH, King and Queen Co., 15 March, 1797; 10 April, 1798. Daughter Mary Brown; granddaughter Sally Dunlop; grandson Charles Brown; gd. dau. Mary Browne; gd. dau. Priscilla Browne; friend James Webb; Mrs. Hannah Campbell; grandson James Campbell. Exrs. Newman Brockenbrough and James Webb.

CATLETT, JOHN, Gloucester Co., 3 May, 1808; 4 July, 1808. Son Charles; son John Walker Carter; dau. Hetty; Bartholomew Yates husband of my dau. Sally. Exrs. William Jones and bro. George Catlett. Wit. W. Taliaferro, Daniel Duvall, Catesby Jones.

WILLIAMSBURG WILLS

CARTER, JAMES, City of Williamsburg, 28 Feb., 1794; 1 Dec., 1794. Wife Sarah; dau. Elizabeth now an infant; niece Charlotte Dickson dau. of Mary Dickson; Amy wife of Benj. Lester; my nephew Dr. Thomas Carter; Rev. John Bracken; Robert Saunders; Elizabeth Saunders. Exrs. Rev. John Bracken, Joseph Prentis and Robert Saunders. Wit. Robert Greenhone, James Davenport.

CLARKE, ROBERT, SNR., Essex Co., 6 April, 1790; 18 Oct., 1790. Wife Margaret; sons Robert and Spencer; dau. Patsy; granddaughter Peggy Brooks; granddaughters Betsey and Peggy Greenwood. Exrs. sons Thomas and Robert, and John Montague. Wit. John Montague, William Simco, John Sadler.

COBB, MICHAEL, Southampton Co., 10 Nov., 1795; 10 Dec., 1795. Brothers Benjamin, Thomas and George Cobb; my youngest child Jack; my wife. Exrs. brother Exum Cobb, Spencer Pierce and Charles Briggs, Jnr. Wit. William Hines, George Clements, Rebecca Mecom.

COLLIER, MOODY, Southampton Co., 13 March, 1815; 18 Dec., 1815. Daughter Eliz. Cosby; dau. Mary A. Davis; dau. Elvira Ann Holt Collier; son Thomas R. Collier. Exrs. my wife, son Thomas and Charles Butts. Wit. Thomas B. Ellis, John Scarborough, Eliz. Moore, Eliz. Clinch.

COCKE, ALLEN, Surry Co., 1 Aug., 1802; 23 Nov., 1802. To sister Anne Hunt Bradley plantation called Bacon's Castle and she to be extx.; friend Robert Hunnicutt, Snr; friend James Simpson. Wit. James Simpson, Saml. Allen, Wm. Randolph, Jnr., P. H. Adams.

COCKE, HENRY, Par. of Southwark, Surry Co., 6 July, 1776; 27 May, 1777. Wife Katherine; sons David, Henry and Lemuel; my late father Lemuel Cocke; dau. Katherine. Exrs. wife and sons David and Lemuel Cocke, Augustine Willis, Wm. Harris, Thomas Harris and Thomas Peete. Wit. John Cargill, James Larke, Thos. Peete, Wm. Parker.

WILLIAMSBURG WILLS

COLLIER, HENRY, Par. of Southwark, Surry Co., 30 May, 1777; 22 July, 1777. Wife Dinah; dau. Ann wife of John Marks of Henrico; dau. Martha wife of Arthur Forster of Southampton; dau. Sarah wife of Wm. Bailey of Surry; dau. Rebecca wife of Joseph Cheatham of Surry. Exrs. Joseph Cheatham and John Marks. Wit. Wm. Simmons, Littleberry Dewell, John Collier, Faith Dewell.

COBB, JOHN, Par. of Nottoway, Southampton Co., 1 Oct., 1792; 8 Nov., 1792. Sons Exum, Michael, Jeremiah, Benjamin, Thomas and Geo. Brow Cobb; dau. Rebecca Mecom wife of Samuel Mecom; grandson Mathew Mecom; granddaughter Polly Mecom; dau. Elizabeth Wooton; granddaughter Jane Exum Wooton. Exrs. Wm. Hems, son Michael and Thomas Gray. Wit. Lucy Lane, Richard Pond, Snr., Drewry Pond.

COBB, BENJAMIN, Southampton Co., 15 Feb., 1823; 20 Nov., 1826. Wife Susanna; nephew Benjamin son of Jeremiah Cobb; Louisa Cobb dau. of my decsd. bro. George B. Cobb; James, Elizabeth and Georgiana R. Cobb children of decd. bro. George B. Cobb. Exr. brother Jeremiah Cobb. No wit.

CRICHTON, WILLIAM, Southampton Co., 19 Dec., 1793; 20 April, 1801. Sons John and James; dau. Susannah Cook; friend Eliz. Dunn. Exrs. Thomas Edmunds and my two sons. Wit. Willis Woodly, Thomas Butts, Elizabeth Eley.

CLOPTON, ROBERT, Cumberland Co., 17 April, 1783; 22 April, 1793. Brothers Reuben, John and George, and sisters Anne Lane Meredith, and Sarah Clopton to divide my land in counties of Prince Edward, Albemarle and Amherst; my mother. Exrs. brothers George and Reuben. Wit. John Brown, Nicholas Peay, Mary Parish, Wm. Clopton, Snr.

COLEMAN, SAMUEL, Norfolk Borough, 28 March, 1805. Wife Sarah all the lot and houses on which her father resided and which was devised to her mother Sukey Maclean by her grandfather Thomas Talbot; daus. Susan and Fanny. Wit. John E. Holt, Alex. Whitehead, Thomas Goodwin.

CLEMENTS, PITMAN, Essex Co., 6 Nov. 1778; Pro. 20 Nov., 1778, in Baltimore Co., Md. To brothers William and Henry land in King and Queen Co.; bro. Mace; sister Catherine Clements. Exrs. Robert Payne Waring, Thomas —— and Archibald Ritchie. Wit. Geo. P. Reynolds, William Beard, Ann Russell.

CLEMENTS, HENRY HAGGARD, Par. So. Farnham, Essex Co., 16 May, 1794; 21 July, 1794. Brother Mace, sister Susannah Robinson and her youngest dau.; nephew Henry Robinson; niece Ann Robinson; niece Lucy Robinson; niece Polly Robinson; James Daingerfield. Exrs. John Daingerfield, Capt. Thos. Dix, Wm. Latane and bro. Mace Clements. Wit. John Brockenbrough, Francis Brooke, W. Taliaferro, Jnr.

CRAIG, EBENEZER, Princess Anne Co., 10 March, 1809; 1 May, 1809. Wife Mary; to Robert Dykes and the sons of my cousin James Page, viz.: James, Alexander and John Craig Page. Exrs. William Warden and William C. Holt. Wit. John Woodard, Wm. Lorey, Jr., Wm. Lorey, Sr., Martin Cummins.

CRICHLOW, JOHN, Town of Jerusalem, Southampton Co., 15 Feb., 1815; 20 Sept., 1819. Wife Mary B. Crichlow; son John to be educated for the profession of medicine; son James to be brought up to the profession of law. Exr. wife. Wit. Wm. B. Goodwyn, Mathew Calvert.

CORRIE, HANNAH, Richmond Co., 4 July, 1791; 2 Jan., 1792. Son Peter Rust; granddaughters Ailcey Lee and Lettis Lee Rust. Exr. son Peter. Wit. John Weathers, Rebecca B. Weathers.

CRUTCHER, THOMAS, Drysdale Par., Caroline Co., 11 Jan., 1782; 1 Feb., 1786. Son John; son Thomas Crutcher of Spotsylvania 75 acres purchased of Gawin Corbin; the representatives of my son Hugh's estate late of Culpepper Co.; son Leonard; son Henry; dau. Margaret Tureman and the children of her decd. husband Charles Tureman; dau. Mary Sneed; dau. Elizabeth Petts; dau. Sarah Crutcher; grandsons Thomas and Sebert Crutcher sons of my decd. son William. Exrs. wife Sarah, son Thomas of Spotsylvania, and son-in-law Israel Sneed of Caroline Co. Codicil, Nephew Henry Crutcher; son-in-law Lunsford Pitts and grandson Thomas to be executors. No wit.

COOK, JOHN, Shipwright, Town of St. Michael, Island of Barbadoes, 6 Dec., 1764; 20 April, 1765. Daughter Sarah land in town of Norfolk, Prov. of Va.; nephews John Newton Cook and George Cook sons of my deced. brother Robert; to John Cook the reputed son of Jane Brisell now an infant at school in Liverpool, Gt. Britain; cousin John Tucker and his partner Samuel Bedford of the Island of Barbadoes, merchants, together with my daughter Sarah to be exrs., as well as my cousin Robert Tucker, Esq., of Norfolk, Va., and friend Goodrich Boush. Wit. Paul Taylor, Robert Arnoll, Wm. Thompson.

COOKE, MORDECAI, JR., Ware Par., Gloucester Co., 25 July, 1769; 5 Apl., 1776. Mother Mrs. Sarah Throckmorton; Warner, Mordecai and Sarah Throckmorton my half bros. and sister, children of Col. Robert Throckmorton; Ann Finnie dau. of William and Eliz. Finnie of York Co. Exr. Col. Robert Throckmorton. Wit. Charles Robinson, Robert Throckmorton, Wm. Mason.

COCKE, HARTWELL, Surry Co., 29 May, 1772; 25 Aug., 1772. Sons John Hartwell, Benjamin, Robert and Richard Cocke; daus. Mary, Martha, Ann and Elizabeth Cocke; wife Ann. Exrs. son John Hartwell Cocke and brother-in-law

WILLIAMSBURG WILLS

Robert Ruffin. Wit. William Browne, David Donnon, Thomas Fenner.

CRUMP, CHARLES, New Kent Co., 4 Feb., 1809; 13 Apl., 1809. Bartlet, Pleasant, Norborn, Sheldon, Hiram and Betsy Crump. Exrs. Bartlet Crump and Nancy McManners. Wit. Wm. Clopton, Judith Peers, James McManners.

CRUMP, BENEDICT, New Kent Co., 9 July, 1811; 10 Oct., 1811. Sons Beverley and Abner; dau. Susanna; my other children; my wife. Exrs. Beverley Crump, Benedict Crump, Geo. P. Crump and Abner Crump. Wit. Francis Ferguson, Thomas Moore.

COOPER, JOHN, James City Co., 15 Dec., 1791; 14 Feb., 1792. To niece Mary and her husband William Browne, land in New Kent Co.; to John and William Browne, and John and William Hankin; to John Cooper Allen son of William Allen by his first wife Susanna; to Mary and her husband William Walker; to Thomas son of John Cowles; to Susanna Gaddy; to Mary Richardson; to Edmund Cowles; remainder of estate to the nephews and nieces of my wife Susanna, viz.; Thomas, Henry, James, Samuel, Sarah and Betsy, sons and daughters of Thomas Cowles, Elizabeth Taylor and John Cowles. Exr. William Browne. Wit. Wm. Richardson, John Browne, Richard Bray, Sarah Browne, Allen Richardson.

CLAYTON, WILLIAM, Clerk of New Kent Co., 10 June, 1797; 14 Dec., 1797. Son William Beverley Clayton; son-in-law Philip Davis; granddaughter Catherine Clayton; son-in-law Armistead Russell; granddaughter Eliz. Armistead Russell; dau. Mary Ann Davis; dau. Elvira Russell. Exr. son Wm. B. Clayton. Wit. John Christian, Benjamin Crump, John H. Christian.

DENNIS, WILLIAM M., James City Co., 22 May, 1820; 13 Feb., 1821. Friend Jesse Cole of Williamsburg and his son Robert; wife Susan E. Dennis; David son of John Minge of

19

WILLIAMSBURG WILLS

Charles City; residue of my wife's father's estate to her son Wm. F. S. Pierce. Exrs. Jesse Cole, John Minge, Common Council of Williamsburg and Board of Trustees at that time for the Charity School of Charles City Co. No wit.

DULIN, MARTHA, Par. of Ware, Gloucester Co., 2 Jan., 1807; 1 May, 1809. Daughter Aphia Dulin and granddaughter Kitty dau. of John Gutree. Wit. Robert Stubblefield, Thomas Stubblefield, Francis D. Jones.

DICKERSON, JOHN, York Hampton Par., York Co., 8 June, 1801; 21 Sep., 1801. Sister Elizabeth Chapman; niece Mary D. Moody; nephew Wm. Chapman; Martha Vaughan; Eliza dau. of John Power; Lucy Barsham; Mary Hyde; Edward Power; Nathaniel Burwell, Jr.; John Waller; Washington son of Edward Power. Exrs. wife Mary and nephew William Chapman. Codicil, 7 July, 1801, alters exrs. to Robert Sheild and John Bryan. Wit. John W. Waller, John Slaughter.

DAVIS, STAIGE, Middlesex Co., 8 Dec., 1812; 22 March, 1813. Eldest dau Maria and second dau. Lucy; daus. Louisa, Elizabeth and Catherine; youngest dau. Martha; sons John A., George S., and James H. Davis. Exrs. my wife and Dr. Anthony Gardner. Wit. Moore G. Fauntleroy, Cary K. Dudley, Henry Dunn.

DAVIS, MARY ANN, New Kent Co., 10 Jan., 1809; 9 March, 1809. Daughter Mary Ann; dau. Rebecca; dau. Catherine Gwatkins. Exrs. Wm. H. Macon and my brother Wm. B. Clayton. Wit. William Holt, Henry Holt.

DAVIS, ELIZ. M., Middlesex Co., 22 Dec., 1820; 27 Feb., 1821. John A. Davis as trustee; dau. Maria G. Braxton; Dr. Anthony Gardner decd.; son James Henry Davis; children Lucy, Louisa, Eliza, John, Catherine and Martha; George S. McIntire infant son of my dau. Louisa A. McIntire. Exrs. John A. Davis and John Chowning, Jr. Wit. Mary Garland, Thomas Boswell.

WILLIAMSBURG WILLS

DAVENPORT, JAMES, Par. of Cople, Westmoreland Co., 13 Apl., 1775; 26 Aug., 1777. Wife sole extx. No wit.

DRINKARD, WM. R., Charles City Co., 29 Dec., 1804; 16 May, 1805. Wife Polly C.; dau. Mary B. Harwood; daus. Betsy and Polly Cocke Drinkard; sons William H., George Joseph, John and David; daus. Agnes Coatney and Nancy Allen; refers to wife's former husband. Exr. Hamlin Willcox. Wit. Christopher P. Dean, M. Willcox.

DUDLEY, GEORGE E., Mathews Co., 20 March, 1814; 9 May, 1814. Son George Mortimer Dudley; my mother; sister Fanny Gibson; Richard Gregory, Snr.,of Georgia; Armistead and John sons of John Cary of Georgia; Edwin son of Edwin Lee of Norfolk; sister Eliz. T. Jones. Exr. Thomas Ransone. Wit. Thomas R. Yeatman, Thomas Ransone, Martha Ayres.

DANDRIDGE, BARTHOLOMEW, New Kent Co., 16 March, 1785; 13 May, 1785. Mother Frances Dandridge; son John; present wife Mary and her mother Lucy Burbidge; sons Julius Burbidge, Bartholomew and William; daus. Martha, Mary and Frances Dandridge; granddaughter Elizabeth Dandridge Claiborne; Exrs. John Lacy, William Armistead, sons John and Julius Dandridge and son-in-law Wm. Dandridge Claiborne. No wit.

DANIEL, FRANCES, Middlesex Co., 16 Oct., 1794; 28 Jan., 1808. Catherine Dillard; Lewis son of Edmund Berkeley; Elizabeth dau. of Edmund Berkeley; niece Anna Curtis. Exr. nephew Thomas Roane. Wit. Cary Kemp, Christ. Robinson, Catherine Dillard.

DUVAL, WILLIAM, Petsworth Par., Gloucester Co., 7 Aug., 1783; 5 May, 1785. Son William; son Francis and his dau. Elizabeth; grandson Samuel Duval; dau. Elizabeth Baker; dau. Mary Hall; son-in-law Michael Pointer husband of my dau. Sarah and their son William; dau. Ellis Stubbs;

WILLIAMSBURG WILLS

children of son-in-law Daniel New; son Samuel. Exrs. sons William and Francis Duval. Wit. John Berry, James Wortham, John Keiningham.

DIACK, ALEXANDER (nuncupative), 3 April, 1789; proved at Norfolk 22 June, 1789. Leaves all to the estate of William Aitchinson of Norfolk.

DOBYNS, WINIFRED, Farnham Par., Richmond Co., 16 April, 1798; 2 Sept., 1801. Rev. Henry Toler of Cople Parish, Westmoreland Co., residuary legatee. Exrs. Rev. Henry Toler, Rev. Samuel Templeman and Ransdale Pierce all of Westmoreland. Wit. Jemima Davis, Peggy Davis, Ann Fauntleroy.

DOBYNS, DANIEL, Richmond Co., 15 Jan., 1784; 3 May, 1784. Son Daniel; son-in-law Joseph Davenport; daus. Caty, Frances, Winifred, Alice, Nancy and Betty. Wit. Daniel Miskell, John Davis, LeRoy Dobyns, Richd. Packet.

DREW, SARAH, Southampton Co., 10 Jan., 1807; 17 Aug., 1807. Nephews James and Robert sons of Bromfield Ridley; nephew Benjamin son of James Blunt; nephew James son of William Ridley; niece Rebecca Massenburg; niece Elizabeth Blunt. Exrs. nephew James Ridley, Snr., Samuel Blunt, Wm. Massenburg. Wit. Benjamin Delk, Elizabeth Delk.

ELLIOTT, CALEB, Essex Co., 3 Sept., 1789; 19 June, 1797. Sons Wiatt and William; grandson John Pitts; wife Margaret. Exrs. sons Wiatt and William. Wit. Wm. F. Gray, Reuben Cleft.

EPPES, LEWELLIN, Westover Par., Charles City Co., 9 Nov., 1755; 3 May, 1758. Son Temple; granddaughter Angelica Wilkinson; grandson Joseph son of Littlebury Royall; wife Angelica; son Peter; daus. Elizabeth, Ann, Mary and Angelica. Extx. wife. Wit. Wm. Watkins, Jr., Richard Royall, William Royall.

WILLIAMSBURG WILLS

ELEY, WILLIAM, Nansemond Co., 12 May, 1779; 14 Feb., 1791. Wife Anne; dau.-in-law Betsey Best; Fredk. Hall; dau.-in-law Anne Best; dau. Catherine Best. Exrs. wife and daus. Betsey and Anne. Wit. Thomas Cowlin, Margaret Cowling, Mary Bradley, Jr.

EDMONSON, THOMAS, Essex Co., 20 Dec., 1757; 17 Dec., 1759. Wife Hannah; sons John, James and William; daus. Sarah, Dorothy and Judith; wife's late father Col. William Todd; sister Eliz. Haye. Exrs. Col. Francis Smith, Col. William Daingerfield, Mordecai Throckmorton, Edmund Pendleton and my son James. Wit. John Burnett, Robert Clacke, Hannah Phillips, Wm. Wright.

EWING, EBENEZER, Falkirk, Co. of Stirling, North Britain, but now for 11 years of Parish of Bristol, York Co., Va., 25 Oct., 1795. To Elizabeth Ashton who is the mother of my son Thomas now living with me; my brothers and sisters; Rev. James Henderson to be guardian to son Thomas. Exrs. John Bryan, Joseph Ferguson, David Miller. Wit. James Southall, Jeremiah Barton, Peter Powell.

ELLIS, SAMUEL, Norfolk Co., 14 Sept., 1797; 16 Oct., 1797. Son Joseph; daus. Christian and Mary; son Hardy; dau. Sarah Fatherly; dau. Keziah Taylor; wife Margaret. Exrs. ——— Wyat: John Bowers. Wit. John Johnson, William Stafford, William Leigh.

ECKLES, SOLOMON, Par. of Cople, Westmoreland Co., 18 March, 1778; 25 March, 1788. Son William alias Spence and Elizabeth Spence my dau.-in-law; son-in-law Thomas Spence; sister Hannah Hall. Exrs. Daniel Bailey, John Moore. Wit. Daniel Bailey, Vincent S. Bailey, James Bailey.

EGGLESTONE, RICHARD, James City Co., 15 May, 1793; 14 April, 1794. Wife Elizabeth and my children. Exrs. wife and Joseph Prentis. Wit. P. Bernard, John Otey, Elizabeth Sculley.

EVANS, WILLIAM, Par. of Nottoway, Southampton Co., 15 March, 1804; 21 May, 1804. Wife Polly A.; son Benjamin; son William. Exrs. wife and Richard E. Williams. No wit.

EDWARDS, WILLIAM, Par. of Southwark, Surry Co., 2 Sept., 1791; 25 April, 1797. Wife Susannah and the child she is now pregnant with; son William; son Thomas the land given me by my uncle William Edwards; son Richard Henry; dau. Ann. Exr. brother Richard Edwards. No wit.

ELLIS, JOSEPH, Norfolk Co., 11 June, 1803; 16 July, 1805. Brother Hardy Ellis; sister Christian Ellis; Stephen Price; Judith Bowers; sister-in-law Rhoda Ellis; Thomas Hare's children; sisters Sarah Fatherly and Keziah Taylor; Margt. Miers. Exrs. Thomas Hare, William Ballentine, Jr. Wit. Charles Ballentine, Robert Bowers, Thomas Collins.

ELLIS HARDY, Norfolk Co. (nuncupative). John Stokes and Robert Fotherdill made oath that Hardy Ellis died in the month of March, 1815, and that it was his desire that his sister Christian Ellis should have his whole estate. Made this 21 March, 1815.

EPPES, PETER, Charles City Co., 29 March, 1763; 7 July, 1773. Son Peter; son John Temple; dau. Elizabeth; dau. Angelica slaves left by my father Lewellin Eppes; father-in-law John Hardyman decd. Exrs. Wm. Royall, Snr., Wm. Royall, Jr., Stith Hardyman. Wit. James Hardyman, William Hardyman. Tr.

FAUSS, MARY, St. Peter's Par., New Kent Co., 24 April, 1788; 11 April, 1793. Son-in-law Thomas Moody; grandfather John Martin, decd.; son Charles Fauss; son John Fauss. Exrs. Joseph Higgins, John Clopton. Wit. John Thomson, James Martin, Elizabeth Davis.

FAUCETT, VINCENT W., Middlesex Co., 23Sept.,1815; 25 Dec., 1815. Nephew James son of Thomas Ferguson in King & Queen Co.; niece Elizabeth Wood dau. of John

WILLIAMSBURG WILLS

Wood; niece Frances Ball. Exrs. Thos. G. Crittenden, Thos. Ferguson Snr. Wit. Sarah C. Crittenden, Martha C. Lewis, Henrietta Ferrell.

FOX, JOHN, of Greenwich, Par. of Petsworth, Gloucester Co., 5 Aug., 1780. My decd. father John Fox, clerk; wife Anne; eldest son John; sons William, Thomas and Henry; dau. Mary Hartwell Fox; dau. Anne Lightfoot Fox; dau. Isabel Catherine Fox. Extx. wife. Wit. Joseph Berkeley, Wm. Purcell, Wm. Rilee.

FILBATES, JOHN, Par. of Westover, Charles City Co., 28 Oct., 1792; 17 Oct., 1811. Children Nancy, Betsey, Polly, Patty and Archibald Filbates; my wife. Wit. Edmund Christian, Charles Evans, James Bates.

FLEET, WILLIAM, St. Stephen's Par., King & Queen Co., 20 April, 1763; 11 Oct., 1773. Sons John and William; land in Orange Co. to son Edwin; daus. Mary Ann and Elizabeth; grandmother Mrs. Eliz. Marriot; friend Col. Humphrey Hill; wife Susannah. Exrs. brother Edwin Fleet, John Semple. Wit. Charles Mortimer, Arthur Hopes, George Eubank, Wm. Birch.

FLEET, EDWIN, King & Queen Co., 27 April, 1778; 13 July, 1778. Nephew Baylor son of Wm. Fleet decd.; nephew Edwin son of Wm. Fleet decd; nephew Henry son of Wm. Fleet decd.; nephew William son of Robert Dudley decd.; bro. John Fleet. Exrs. William Dudley, Henry Fleet. Wit. James Jones, John Jones, Molly Jones.

FARLEY, SIMON, Gent., Island of Antigua., 13 June, 1756; 18 June, 1756. My wife; son Francis; daus. Elizabeth, Rebecca, Ann; son John lands in Virginia and North Carolina; uncles Robert Christian and Mathew Christian; bro. Francis Farley. Wit. John Halliday, Alex. Crawford, John D. Murphy. Proved before His Excellency, George Thomas,

25

Esq., Capt. Genl. and Governor in Chief over His Majesty's Leeward Carribbee Islands.

GARDNER, JOHN, King & Queen Co., 1 June, 1784; 13 Sept., 1784. Wife Mary; Ann Field dau. of Stephen Field; dau. Eliz. Macon Gardner; brother Anthony Gardner and sister Eliz. Row. Exrs. Major Thomas Row and my wife. Codicil same date, mentions his first wife, Eliz. Field, and her bro. Stephen Field. Wit. Geo. Didlake, Wm. Dillard, Jr., Robert Didlake.

GEORGE, FREDERICK, Nansemond Co., 16 May, 1810; 14 Dec., 1812. Wife Nancy; Thomas Beavan; my grandchildren Elizabeth, George, and George Thomas Beavan; grandson Wm. George Cowling; grandson Jesse Cowling. Extx. wife. Wit. Kedar Webb, Mary Smith, Jane Yeamans, Thos. Claiborne. Codicil 16 July, 1811. Appoints John C. Cohoon and Kedar Webb as trustees. Wit. Richd. Godwin, Lillias Godwin, Molly Smith. 2d codicil 17 April, 1812.

GOODE, EDWARD, Caroline Co., 28 March, 1763; August Court, 1763. Wife Martha and my four cihldren Ann, Richard, Edmund and Martha. Exr. Thomas Ship. Wit. Richard Goode, Betty Branghile.

GARNETT, JAMES, Gent., Essex Co., 25 Dec., 1765; 15 July, 1765. Grandsons Francis, Henry and Augustine Garnett; to son Muscoe land in Spottsylvania, Orange and Caroline Counties; son James; daus. Betty and Sarah; granddaughter Milly Garnett; my wife. Son Muscoe to be extr. and guardian to son James and dau. Betty. Wit. Al. Rose, James Andrews, David Pitts.

GREGORY, JOHN, JR., Charles City, 3 Dec., 1776; 3 Sept., 1777. Wife Martha; children Richmond and John Mumford Gregory. Exrs. wife, Wm. Green Munford, Richmond Terrell, Wm. Terrell and my bro. Wm. Gregory. Wit. Mary Sherman, Sarah Clarke.

WILLIAMSBURG WILLS

GORDON, ANN ISHAM, Prince George Co., 16 Jan., 1790. No date probate. Elizabeth McNeill; William eldest son of late Col. Wm. Yates, and Benj. Poythress Yates his second son; niece Mary Muir and her son Wm. Poythress Muir and her dau. Margaret Muir; Lucy dau. of John Gordon decd.; friend Thomas Gordon; sister Eliz. Ramsay; Eliz. Peachy. Exrs. Thomas G. Peachy, Thomas Gordon. Wit. Eleanor Crane, Eliz. Milly Fraser, Susannah Cox.

GREEN, PETER, Upper Parish, Nansemond Co., 22 May, 1765; 12 March, 1770. Sons Peter and Thomas; daus. Patience Jones, Elizabeth Green, Sarah Nelm and Prudence Green. Exr. Christopher Roberts. Witnesses: Michael Farrow, John Pinna.

GRAY, EDWIN, Southampton Co., 23 Sept., 1788; 10 June, 1790. Sons Joseph, Thomas, Edwin and Henry; dau. Mary; my wife. Exrs. brother James Gray, my three sons and Sanl. Simmons. Wit. Benj. Ruffin Sr., Benj. Ruffin Jr., Saml. Kellor.

GODWIN, JOHN, Isle of Wight, 22 Dec., 1789; 7 Jan., 1790. Sons John and Bartley; daus. Elizabeth and Charlotte; wife Silvia. Extr. son John. Wit. Samuel Weston, Copeland Whitefield, Jr., Tabitha Whitley.

GRYMES, PHILIP LUDWELL, of Brandon, Middlesex Co., 23 April, 1805; 24 June, 1805. Wife Judith; my lately decd. son; dau. Jane and her husband Samuel Wm. Sayre; brother Benjamin Grymes; my manager Wm. Wood. Exrs. friend Ralph Wormeley Sr., of Rosegill, Nathaniel Burwell, Sr. and Jr., of Frederick, my nephew Robert Nelson of York and Mann Page of Gloucester. Wit. Akiana M. Curtis, Eliz. Page, Dorothy Churchill, Wm. Wood, Julius C. Pollard.

GARNER, BRADLEY, Westmoreland Co., 13 Oct., 1761; 26 June, 1770. To son George land bought of Samuel Garner;

son Vincent; dau. Eleanor; dau. Hannah Cox; dau. Elizabeth; son Benjamin; daughter Lettice; grandson Thomas Pritich; Rodam Pritich; wife Catherine; son Jeremiah. Exrs. wife, son Benjamin and Peter Cox. Wit. Presley Hall, Aston Hall, John Grace.

GILMOUR, ROBERT, Gent., Lancaster Co., 23 May, 1782. To son John the estate left me by my grandfather at Neatherton, Kilmarnock, North Britain; son Robert land in Frederick County, and land in town of Kilmarnock; my wife. Exrs. Col. James Ball, Dr. William Ball, David Galloway, Jr., John Dean, Mungo Harvey.

GILCHRIST, JOHN, physician, Borough of Norfolk, 23 Nov., 1799; 27 July, 1801. Friend Dr. Philip Barrand; sisters Elizabeth Kelly and Frances Fitt, now residents in the Island of Bermuda; my relative St. George Tucker of Williamsburg; mentions his mother and her second marriage (no names). Exrs. St. George Tucker, Dr. Philip Barrand. Wit. Robert Farmar, Wm. Cuthbert, Archibald Campbell.

GWALTNEY, THOMAS, Surry Co., 25 Nov., 1797; 23 Jan., 1798. Son-in-law Benj. Bell; grandson Benj. C. Bell; dau. Sarah Holleman; dau. Rebecca Phillips; dau. Martha Cofer; son-in-law Benj. Shelly; dau. Ann Cofer, dau. Polly Gwaltney; sons Thomas P., and Ludwell Gwaltney; dau. Nancy Gwaltney. Exrs. wife Sarah and son Thomas P. Gwaltney. Wit. John Gwaltney, Joseph Davis, William White.

GRIFFIN, LE ROY, 26 Oct., 1775; Proved Richmond Co., 4 Dec., 1775. To eldest dau. Ann Corbin negroes in Westmoreland County; dau. Elizabeth; youngest daughter Judith. Exrs. wife, brother Thomas B. Griffin, Col. James Ball, William Peachey. Wit. James Selden, John Leland, Thos. Beale, Joseph Dale.

GRAY, MILES W., Isle of Wight Co., 30 Nov., 1819; 4 June, 1821. Sister Elizabeth S., wife of Nathl. Wills; grand-

WILLIAMSBURG WILLS

father Miles Wills decd.; father Josiah Gray decd. Exr. Nathaniel Wills. Wit. William Godwin, Nicholas Waite.

HAYNES, BETTY, Princess Anne Co., 12 May, 1806; 5 Dec., 1808. Daughter Mary wife of Francis Moore; grandson William son of James Haynes; dau. Fanny Haynes; son Henry decd.; granddaughter Betsy Thorogood Moore dau. of Francis Moore. Exr. Mitchell Thorogood. Wit. Thads. Bowman, James Nimmo, W. T. Nimmo.

HARRISON, JOHN, Isle of Wight Co., 1 April, 1790; 7 Feb., 1791. Wife Elizabeth; daus. Harriet, Elizabeth and Woody. Exrs. wife and brother Richard Harrison. Wit. Harewood Callcote, Betsey Harrison.

HORNSBY, WILLIAM, City of Williamsburg, 3 July, 1804; 28 Jan., 1805. To housekeeper Fanny Walker and her daus. Sally, Peggy and Sophia Walker; nephews Joseph and Thomas, sons of my bro. Joseph Hornsby of State of Kentucky. Exrs. Robert Prentis, John Bracken and Joseph Prentis.

HERBERT, JONAS, Par. of St. Brides, Norfolk Co., 22 Feb., 1779; August Court, 1782. Brothers James, Argile, Jonathan and Henry; late bro. Christopher; sister Elizabeth Payne; sister Abigail Hopkins; to Tabitha dau. of bro. Caleb Herbert; to Ann dau. of bro. James Herbert. Exrs. brothers James and Jonathan.

HERBERT, CHRISTOPHER, Norfolk Co., 18 May, 1772; April Court, 1774. Brothers Jonas and Jonathan; my mother; Lydia Causon; bro. James; bro. Henry; sister Abigail Herbert; bro. Caleb. Wit. James Herbert, Saml. Barrington.

HOPKINS, JOSHUA, Princess Anne Co., 9 Aug., 1792; 6 July, 1795. Wife Kezia; son Joshua; dau. Jennet and her husband Wm. G. Knight; dau. Elizabeth and her husband John Owens; dau. Rebecca and her husband John Armstrong; grandson Joshua Armstrong; grandson Joshua Hopkins; dau.

Nancy Hopkins. Exrs. wife and son Joshua. Wit. Hilary Moseley Sr., Joseph Edmonds, Tully Moseley.

HOLT, WILLIAM (No place given.), 11 Jan., 1791. Wife Peachy; son Daniel; dau. Elizabeth Coleman; sons William and David; son Samuel estate in Charles City; daus. Jane and Mary. Exrs. wife, Wm. Russell, Robert Greenhow, Wm. Coleman.

HEFFERNAN, HENRY, Par. of Christ Church, Middlesex Co., 14 Feb., 1814; 28 Feb., 1814. Carter D. Berkeley; Lewis Berkeley; Edward Pribble, who was adopted by me; Maria dau. of Elliott Muse. Exrs. Philip Grymes, Elliott Muse. Wit. George M. McIntire, James R. Steptoe.

HARWOOD, WILLIAM, City of Williamsburg, 11 May, 1793; 6 Oct., 1794. Sisters Sarah and Lucy Harwood. Exrs. brother Humphrey Harwood, James Galt.

HARVEY, MUNGO, Washington Par., Westmoreland Co., 28 Feb., 1794; 29 April, 1794. Sons James and John; daus. Ann, Sarah and Elizabeth. Exrs. wife and son James. Wit. John Fox, Thomas Landrum.

HILL, FRANCES, Isle of Wight Co., 4 June, 1788; 5 Sept., 1791. Son Joseph; dau. Elizabeth wife of John Harrison and the latter to be extr. Wit. Samuel Bidgood, Benjamin Tynes, Elizabeth Hill.

HENRY, JAMES, Northumberland Co., 9 March, 1801; 9 Sept., 1805. Wife Sarah; son Edward; Mr. John Wise of Accomac the husband of my dau. now decd., and his two sons George and John Wise; Maria dau. of my son-in-law Hancock Eustace of Stafford Co.; dau. Elizabeth wife of Wm. Moncure; James son of my decd. son 'Samuel H. Henry, and Charles Seaburgh Henry son of the said James Henry and Mary Henry his mother; son John land in Pittsylvania and Halifax counties. Exrs. sons Edward and John Henry, John Wise, Wm. Moncure.

WILLIAMSBURG WILLS

HENOP, MARY, Norfolk Co., 13 Oct., 1820; 20 Nov., 1820. Dau.-in-law Frances wife of John W. Henop; grandchildren Frederick Lewis Henop and Catherine S. Henop; mentions Col. Ludwick Wettner decd., of whom "I am the dau. and sole heir at law." Exr. son Philip Henop. Wit. James Peed, Eliza A. Parker, Robert Brough.

HERRING, DANIEL, Isle of Wight Co., no date. Pro. 10 May, 1823. Niece Martha Hatton and her husband John, and her son Daniel Hatton; Aurora wife of George Lankford, who moved to Ky.; Eliza dau. of James Bridger. (No witnesses and will is unsigned.

HOLT, JOHN, Surry Co., 6 Feb., 1782; 28 Jan., 1783. Sons John and Rowland; my wife; brother Josiah Holt; my daughters. Exrs. Nicholas Faulcon Jr., Wm. Clinch Jr., Jacob Faulcon, Christopher Clinch and my two sons. Wit. Wm. Spratley, Wm. Boyce, Carter Crafford, Wm. Clinch, Michl. Blow.

HILL, JOSEPH, Par. of Newport, Isle of Wight Co., 29 Oct., 1775; 4 Jan., 1776. Son Joseph; daus. Mary and Eliz. Hill; wife Frances. Exr. son Joseph. Wit. Francis Young, Jesse Herring, John Woodley.

HARWOOD, HUMPHREY, SR., City of Williamsburg and Co. of York, 5 Aug., 1788; 20 April, 1789. Son William land in James City Co.; son Humphrey. Exrs. son William and Robert Anderson.

HOLDEN, GEORGE, Ware Parish, Gloucester Co., 2 Jan., 1777; 5 June, 1777. Daughters Anna and Susannah; the children of my sister Eliz. and her husband Wm. Taliaferro; my wife. Exrs. James Hubard of Williamsburg, and John Perrin and Isaac Smith of Accomack. Wit. Robert Jannis, Eliz. Willis, Mary Mason Booth, Christopher Page.

HANKINS, JOHN, James City, 3 April, 1799; 14 Dec., 1801. To Eliz. Harman, Martha Greenhow, Benj. Allen and Eliz. Butler Allen, children of my friend Wm. Allen (called Lindsay), and the latter to be extr.; my wife. Wit. Robert Sanford, Jesse Lindsay, Wm. Lindsay, Minitree Orrell. Codicil dated 14 March, 1801, mentions death of his wife.

IRWIN, BEDFORD MORRIS, Warwick Co., 8 May, 1774; 8 April, 1779. Wife Frances; dau. Eliz. Jones Irwin; son John Jones Irwin. Exr. Edward Baptist. (Wife Frances renounced all interest in the will of her decd. husband under date 12 Jan., 1775.) Wit. Frances Lee, Wm. Rowan.

IRBY, HARDYMAN, Charles City Co., 2 June, 1798; 19 July, 1798. Son Lightfoot; son Henry B.; dau. Betsy. Exrs. Honl. John Tyler and Mr. Francis H. Dancy. Wit. Wm. T. Ballard, M. McLaran, John Royster.

JONES, PHILIP EDWARDS, Mathews Co., 24 April, 1801; 8 June, 1801. Dau. Fanny wife of James Gibson, the latter to be exr. Wit. James Jones, Johanna Jones, Wm. Hodges.

JONES, FRANCIS, Nansemond Co., but at present in town of Portsmouth, 28 Nov., 1806; 8 Dec., 1806. Friend Capt. John Brooks of Portsmouth; John son of Wm. King of Portsmouth; Rosanna Amelia Dashiell, dau. of Dr. Fisher Dashiell of Nansemond Co. Exrs. Col. Wm. Wilkinson and John Godwin former Sheriff of Nansemond Co. Wit. S. Whitehead, Wm. King, John Brooks, Wm. Wilkinson.

JONES, THOMAS, Southampton Co., 20 May, 1799; 21 July, 1800. Wife Sally; dau. Hannah Briggs; dau. Rebecca Williamson. Exrs. wife, James Gee and Saml. Edmonds. Wit. Henry Blunt, Nathl. Edwards, John Whitehead.

JONES, SARAH, Southampton Co., 21 Sept., 1798; 15 Oct., 1798. Mother-in-law Eliz. Jones; my decd. husband Charles B. Jones; Ann and Eliz. B. Jones daus. of said Eliz. Jones; Hannah B. and Rebecca W. Jones daus. of

WILLIAMSBURG WILLS

Thomas Jones; Susanna Drew; Sarah Norfleet Blunt, dau. of Wm. Blunt; mother Mary Gee; Lavinia Norfleet Gee dau. of my father-in-law James Gee. Exrs. uncle John Wilkinson and father-in-law James Gee. Wit. Martha Williamson, Henry Coker, James Wilkinson.

JOYNE, ABEL, Accomack Co., 18 Dec., 1781; 30 July, 1782. Wife Anne; Priscilla wife of Jesse Watson; daus. Susanna, Margaret and Mary. Exrs. wife, Arthur Downing, Elijah Watson. Wit. Thomas Underhill, Eleazar Core.

JAMES, JOHN, James City Co., 3 Feb., 1818; 9 March, 1818. Sons Thruston, John and Geo. W. James; daus. Elizabeth and Susan. Exrs. Archibald Hawkins and son Thruston James. Wit. Edwd. Richardson, Allen Richardson, Wm. R. Richardson.

JARVIS, WILLIAM, York Co., 11 Aug., 1824; 15 Nov., 1824. Wife Mary; sons Thomas and John; daus. Mary and Fanny; my grandchildren. Exrs. Richard R. Corbin, Henry Edloe. Wit. Wm. T. Galt, Nicholas Ennis.

JONES, JOHN, Par. of Ware, Gloucester Co., 14 Sept., 1750; 25 Apl., 1751. Wife Ann; dau. Elizabeth. Exrs. wife and John Cooke. Wit. Jonathan Hodges, Robert Beard.

KENNON, ANN, Chesterfield Co., 24 July, 1766; Sept. Court, 1769. Daughters Ann and Mary lands in Chesterfield; my decd. husband; sons William and John. Exrs. Col. Theodrick Bland, Col. John Banester. Wit. Susan Burton, Ann Hunt Hall, William Burton.

KELLY, JOHN, Sussex Co., 20 Oct., 1789; 1 April, 1790. Son John; wife Elizabeth; children Patty, Lucretia, Elizabeth and Anna Kelly, and Sally Tanner. Exrs. wife and son John. Wit. John Huson, Wm. Wynne, Ann Huson, Edward Wyatt.

KER, DAVID, Middlesex Co., 31 July, 1772. Sister Christian; wife Frances and the child she now goes with. Exrs.

33

Honl. Richard Corbin, James Gregory. Wit. Joanna Tucker, Sarah Hearn, Robert Spratt, Wm. Jeffries.

KING, JOHN, Borough of Norfolk, 20 Oct., 1783; 16 Jan., 1784. Wife Ann; sons Bolling, Miles and John. Exrs. wife, Bolling Starke and brother Miles King.

KING, MILES, SNR., Borough of Norfolk, 5 Aug., 1812; 27 Feb., 1815. Son Miles land in Georgia; daughters Elizabeth, Cary and Custine; grandson Robert Donaldson Thorburn; grandson Miles King. Exrs. wife and son Miles King.

KEMP, THOMAS, Middlesex Co., 10 Oct., 1772; 28 Dec., 1772. Daughters Mary, Anne and Hannah; wife Mary; sons Cary, Peter, Thomas and Matthew; Oswald Smith. Exrs. wife, James Mills and Geo. Lorimer. Wit. James Gregory, Matthew Fearn, Wm. Jones, Robert Kemp.

KELSICK, ELIZABETH, Princess Anne Co., 22 April, 1779; 22 June, 1789. Daughter Eleanor Moseley; dau. Frances Robinson; dau. Isabella. Exrs. sons-in-law Alex. Moseley and Tully Robinson. Wit. Edward Hack Moseley, Jr.

KELLS, RICHARD, Southampton Co., 25 May, 1789; 14 Jan., 1790. Daughter Mary Cocke; sons Samuel and Richard. Exr. son Samuel. Wit. Benj. Parker, Richard Cocke, Jr.

KEENE, NEWTON, Gent., St. Stephens Par., Northumberland Co., 26 Nov., 1770; 12 Aug., 1771. My wife; son Thomas land in Faixfax Co.; sons Newton and John land in Loudoun Co. Exrs. eldest son William Keene, David Boyd, Richd. Lee, Matthew Neale. Wit. Jeane Garner, John Blincoe.

LASHLY, MARY, Sussex Co., 27 Aug., 1794; 4 June, 1795. James Jones; Robert Jones; Thomas Bishop; Nancy Briggs.

WILLIAMSBURG WILLS

Exrs. James and Robert Jones. Wit. James Clary, Eliz. Lashly.

LASHLY, WILLIAM, Sussex Co., 15 Jan., 1788; 18 Sept., 1788. Wife Mary; sister Eliz. Lashly; Jesse Casely; Hartwell Casely. Exrs. wife and Samuel Jones. Wit. James B. Jones, Robert Jones, John H. Barker.

LEIGH, RICHARD, Petsoe Par., Gloucester Co., 31 Dec., 1799; 7 April, 1800. Eldest son Thomas Rowe Leigh; son Ferdinand; son Wm. Richard Leigh; my wife. Exrs. John Hughes, John Catlette. Wit. Thomas Jones, Jesse White, Horatio G. Harwood.

LESTER, BENJAMIN, York Co., 26 Sept., 1794; 15 June, 1795. Wife Amy and all my children. Exrs. wife and her brother Joshua Morris and John Goodall. Wit. Thomas Minson, Christopher Curtis, Judy Wright.

LIGHTFOOT, NICHOLAS, James City Co., 3 June, 1806; 11 Dec., 1809. To my two favorite boys of color William and George and their mother Isabella, all of whom I have freed. Exrs. Peter Robert Deneufville of Williamsburg, Wm. Harkins of York Co., and Francis Pigott of James City Co. Wit. John Cooke, Peter Powell, Josias Moody.

LEWIS, JOHN, City of Williamsburg, 13 Aug., 1785; 10 Oct., 1785. Wife Betty; daus. Anne, Betty and Mary; bros. William, David and Charles; my brothers and sisters in Great Britain. Exrs. wife, John Ambler and my three brothers. Wit. J. Prentis, Jesse Cole, Samuel Dixon.

LOWRY, JOHN, Elizabeth City Co., 29 Jan., 1786; 28 Jan., 1790. Sons John, Thomas, Robert and Edmund; daus. Nancy, Frances, Molly and Jenny; brother William Lowry. Extrs. wife, son William, George Booker, Richard Brown. Wit. Westwood Armistead, Benj. Byan.

LANGSTONE, MARY, York Co., 4 June, 1790; 15 Dec., 1794. Daughter Sarah Hunt; son-in-law John Budsong

Hunt. Exr. Nicholas Presson. Wit. Hinde Russell, William Howard, Francis Howard.

LAWRENCE, MILLS, Isle of Wight Co., 15 Sept., 1814; 4 March, 1816. Wife Martha; nephew John Lawrence land in Southampton Co.; Mills Bridger son of Joseph Bridger; William son of Joseph Ballard; Lawrence son of Robert Ely; Edwin son of said Robert and his other sons Mills, Gilbert and Benjamin; Esther dau. of Temply Holloway; Penelope Holloway dau. of Thomas; James son of Joseph Bridger; William and Caty children of Joseph Bridger; Nanny dau. of Joseph Ballard; Elisha son of Joseph Ballard; Joseph, Jr., Margaret and Atteline Ballard children of Joseph Ballard; friend Carr Bowen; Mary Ann Wilson; John Lawrence Bowen son of Carr Bowen; William Everitt Doughtry; nieces Sally Bowen and Peggy Ballard. Exrs. wife and Carr Bowen. Wit. Mills Carr, Jonathan Lankford, Augustus Ballard, Elisha Carr.

MOORE, ELIZABETH, York Co., 29 Dec., 1804. Daughter Susannah Hubbard; sons John and Charles Moore. Exrs. two sons, and son-in-law James Hubbard. Wit. Rebecca Peters, Mathew Hubbard, John B. Inge, William Inge, Zelica Whitaker.

MATTHEWS, JOHN, Kingston Par., Gloucester Co., 1 April, 1766; 5 Feb., 1767. Daughter Dorothy Miller; dau. Ann Scrosby; son Rev. John Matthews; son Richard; son Edward, son Robert; James Scrosby husband of my dau. Ann Scrosby; mentions wife (no name given). Exrs. sons-in-law Thomas Miller and Richard Gregory and son Rev. John Matthews. Wit. Robert Dalgliesh, Ann Jones, John Flippen.

MURRAY, WILLIAM, Par. of Christ Church, Middlesex Co., 9 Dec., 1786; 26 Feb., 1787. Wife Anne; daus. Mary Anne, Harriet and Fanny. Exrs. wife and Col. Peter Kemp. Wit. Samuel Klug, Cary Kemp, Peter Kemp, Charles Curtis.

MUSE, HUDSON, Middlesex Co., 17 April, 1798; 22 July, 1799. Son Thomas land in Middlesex called Hampstead; son Elliott land in Middlesex; late wife Agnes; mentions land that Lawrence Muse got by intermarriage with his wife Jane; land that Thomas Roane got by intermarriage with his wife Molly Neilson; son Neilson Muse lots in Urbana; four daus. Letty, Qulict, Miranda and Cordelia. Exrs. sons Thomas and Elliott Muse. Wit. Lewis Seward, John Muse, James Wortham.

MORRIS, WILLIAM, mariner, Kingston Par., Mathews Co., 23 Dec., 1791; 30 Jan., 1794. Wife Fanny; children of my decd. brother Thomas Morris, viz.: William, Thomas, and Mary Morris now the wife of William Davis, Miller White Morris, and Fanny Morris. Exrs. wife and nephew William Morris. Wit. Francis Williams, John Turner.

MORRIS, THOMAS. Extract of a letter admitted to probate in Gloucester Co., 4 April, 1782, and dated Fort Morris, 27 Nov., 1778: "Should it please God to take me off in this contest without seeing you again, my will and pleasure is, that my estate whatever is left to be equally divided with you and the children, yours in haste. (Signed) Thomas Morris." Wit. Rebecca Bacon, John Howell, Mary Leipine.

McGUIRE, EDMUND, Borough of Norfolk, 3 April, 1819; 30 June, 1819. Eugene son of friend Eugene Higgins of Norfolk farm in Norfolk Co.; rest of estate divided between said Eugene and my brother John McGuire now in Ireland. Exr. Eugene Higgins. Wit. Benj. Pollard, Dennis Dawley.

McINTOSH, ROBERT, declaration made to Charles H. Graves and Henry Goffigan on Monday evg., 13 Feb., 1815; probated in Surry Co., 27 March, 1815. Grandson William H. M. Blunt; sons-in-law David Price and William Scammell; dau. Sally Harwood, my wife and all my children. Exrs. David Price and Wm. Scannell. Wit. Charles H. Graves, Henry Goffigan.

WILLIAMSBURG WILLS

MELSON, ISAAC, Accomack Co., 5 June, 1784; 1 June, 1785. Son Levin; daus. Nancy, Betty, Caty and Polly; my wife. Exr. Charles Bagwell. Wit. Peggy Melson, Anne Melson, William Arbuckle.

MUTTER, THOMAS, York Co., 23 Nov., 1811; 20 July, 1812. Wife Anna and my children as they come of age. Exrs. wife, brother John Mutter, friend Gawin S. Corbin, brother-in-law George Southall, Col. Richard Adams. Wit. W. M. Waller, A. D. Galt, Wm. Gilliam.

MELSON, LEVIN, Accomack Co., 31 March, 1795; 29 June, 1795. Wife Nanny; son Noah Wyatt Melson; son James; daus. Amy, Bridget and Rachel. Extx. wife. Wit. Southy Satchell, Jacob Littleton, Susa Littleton.

McINTOSH, RICHARD, Warwick Co., 17 Feb., 1803. Wife Mary; sons Richard and Thomas; children of Sarah Allen, Patsy Prepon and Elizabeth Crandal. Exrs. Thomas and George Mattuote and Samuel McIntosh.

MARSTON, JOHN, Surry Co., 25 Oct., 1797; 27 March, 1798. All estate to wife Susanna, she to be extx. Wit. James Belsches, Jr., Wm. Cocke, James Stewart.

MARRABLE, CHARLES, Par. of Westover, Charles City Co., 4 July, 1776; 4 Nov., 1778. My three daughters Amy Drinkard, Agnes Collier and Martha Major; decd. brother Henry Hartwell Marrable; sons Edward, William, Benjamin, Hartwell, John, George and Abraham Marrable; wife Ann. Exrs. Wm. Edloe, Henry Southall. Wit. William Holdcroft, James Bullifant, Littleberry Perry.

McDONALD, DUNCAN, Borough of Norfolk, 16 Oct., 1806; 31 Oct., 1806. Wife Ann; dau. Ann; Mrs. Catherine Niemeyer; son Daniel; mentions legacy left by Daniel McPherson; dau. Mary; son John. Exrs. wife and John C. Neimeyer. Wit. Martin Doyle, Bernard Mulhollen, John McPhail.

WILLIAMSBURG WILLS

MALLORY, JOHN, Isle of Wight, 30 Dec., 1788; Feb. Court, 1789. Wife Mary; son William; daus. Martha, Mary, Frances, Keziah and Angelina; grandchildren Martha Van Wagner and William Todd. Exrs. wife, son William and son-in-law Samuel Davis. Wit. Davis Day, James Lupo, Richard Todd.

MOORE, JOHN, Elizabeth City Co., 26 April, 1803; 28 July, 1803. My part of Francis Hollier's estate to my children William Augustine, Frances Hollier and Sarah Hollier Moore; wife Sarah and brother William Moore to be exrs. and guardians to my children Mary Shields Moore, Wm. Augustine, Frances H., Sarah H. Moore. Wit. Wm. Seymour, Sr., Roscow Parsons, Robert Seymour.

MARCH, BERNARD, Nansemond Co., 5 Jan., 1815; 13 Feb., 1815. Wife Welthana; sons Bernard, James and John; dau. Margaret Holland; son Dempsey; daus. Mary Ann and Susan. Exrs. wife and son John. Wit. Dempsey Langston, Nancy Hall, Winney March.

MITCHELL, WILLIAM, York Hampton Par., York Co., 12 Feb., 1786; 17 April, 1786. Wife Damaris. Extr. Laurence Gibbons. Wit. John Moss, George Gibbons, Thomas Gibbons.

MORGAN, GEORGE, of the British Consulate for Virginia, and now residing at Norfolk, 10 Aug., 1811; 26 Feb., 1812. The two illegitimate children that I have by Mary Buchanan a free mulatto woman who is aged 18 years, and living in the Borough of Norfolk, viz.: a son Henry born 30 April, 1809, and a dau. Mary Ann Eliza born 28 Sept., 1810. I bequeath to them and their mother the said Mary, five hundred pounds sterling. My sister Harriet Eliza Clarke of Camden Town near London; mentions his mother. Exrs. Thomas Hamilton, Esq., of Queen's Street, Georges Sq., Glasgow, William Henry Thompson and Robert Dickson of Norfolk.

WILLIAMSBURG WILLS

MORGAN, DANIEL, Par. of Cople, Westmoreland Co.,
20 Sept., 1782; 26 Aug., 1789. Nephew Daniel son of my
brother David Morgan; my wife. Exrs. three brothers William, Andrew and Benjamin Morgan. Wit. Wm. McClen-
ahan, Wm. Richards, James Griggs, Wm. Burges.

MITCHELL, RICHARD, Lancaster Co., 14 Feb., 1779;
20 Sept., 1781. Wife Ann; nephews Richard and Robert
Mitchell; Sarah dau. of my nephew Robert Chinn; Susana
Glascock and Hannah Mitchell sisters of Richard and Robert
above named; decd. sister Sarah Chinn; children of my
sister Frances Fauntleroy; sister Judith Glascock. Exrs.
nephews Richard and Robert Mitchell.

MINGE, DAVID, Par. of Westover, Charles City Co., 1
Feb., 1781; 7 Nov., 1781. Daughters Rebecca Jones Minge
and Anne Shields Minge; wife Christina; sons John and
George Hunt Minge; dau. Judith Bray Minge; Sarah Lorton
and Margaret Ross. Exrs. wife and kinsman Freeman
Walker. Wit. Thomas Harwood, John Harwood, Benj. Ed-
mundson.

MACKIE, ANDREW, SNR., Surry Co., 28 June, 1785; 5
July, 1790. Estate to wife and children. Exrs. wife, sons
Andrew, Joseph and John, and friends Archibald Dunlap
and Thomas Janson. Wit. Thomas Forsyth, Zebulon Lewis,
David Cocke.

MINGE, GEORGE, Par. of Westover, Charles City Co.,
19 Sept., 1781; 2 Jan., 1782. Wife Mary; dau. Sarah relict
of Freeman Walker and her children. Exrs. Henry Southall,
Wyatt Walker. Wit. Bernard Major, Ann Willcox.

MILLER, SIMON, Par. St. Ann, Essex Co., 25 April, 1792;
15 Oct., 1792. Son William and his son Simon; grandson
Simon son of Sarah Miller; dau. Elizabeth Stockdell and her
son John; dau. Ann Rennolds and her children, her son Robert
excepted; dau. Isabella Rowzee; dau. Margaret Miller. Exrs.

WILLIAMSBURG WILLS

son William Miller, Wm. Waring, Jr., Robert Baylor. Wit. Reuben Atkinson, James Roy, John T. Washington, John Sale, Robert Gibson.

MILLER, WILLIAM, Par. of St. Ann, Essex Co., 11 Nov., 1792; 15 April, 1793. Wife Susannah; sons Simon, John and William; daus. Kitty and Susannah. Exrs. Capt. Wm. Waring and Capt. Henry Garnett. Wit. James Roy, Edward Mathews, Lovel Pierce. Codicil, 29 Jan., 1793.

MILLS, JAMES, Gent., Middlesex Co., 3 May, 1781; 28 Jan., 1782. Sister Ann Butcher; nephew John Mills; Eliz. Mills Fraser; Miss Eliz. Corrie; Miss Lucy Wortham; Miss Maria Beverley; friend Robert Beverley. Exrs. wife Elizabeth, William Graham, Overton Cosby, James Gregory. Codicil, 24 Sept., 1781, adds the following to the list of exrs. nephew John Mills and Mr. James Ross. Wit. Bennett Brown, Samuel Klug, Harry B. Yates.

MITCHELL, JAMES, King and Queen Co., 4 April, 1794; 9 June, 1794. Son James; Sally widow of my son Nicholas and her son James; dau. Anna Nunn; granddaughters Betsy Hemmingway Mitchell and Polly Clack Mitchell, daus. of my decd. son John; son-in-law Jeremiah Spencer and Mary his wife, land in King William Co. Exr. son James Mitchell. Wit. Robert Pollard, Thomas Bew, John Davenport.

MUNFORD, WM. GREENE, Charles City Co., 8 Feb., 1786; 3 May, 1786. Four sons Robert, John, Stanhope and Wm. Greene Munford; daus. Mary Lightfoot and Elizabeth. Exr. Honl. John Tyler, Esq. Wit. John Gregory, John Marston, Jr., J. Harwood.

NORVELL, WILLIAM, James City Co., 1 Sept., 1802; 13 Dec., 1802. To Armistead Norvell Lightfoot and his brother George B. Lightfoot; Catherine, Elizabeth and George B., children of William and Lucy Lightfoot; Mary wife of Jeremiah Taylor; William and Mary, children of James N.

Walker; William, Mary, Samuel, Catherine and John, children of John and Mary Allen; Park son of William and Elizabeth Goodall. Exrs. William Lightfoot and James Semple. Wit. Leonard Henley, William Richardson.

NELSON, THOMAS, Town and Co. of York, 26 Dec., 1788; 16 Feb., 1789. Wife Lucy; my mother; son Thomas land in Williamsburg and James City; son Philip land in Hanover Co.; son Francis land in Hanover Co.; son Hugh land in Hanover Co., known by the name of York; my brother Hugh Nelson; son Robert land in Hanover known as Montair; dau. Eliza Page; daus. Mary, Lucy, Susanna and Judith Nelson; mentions Dr. Augustine Smith; nephew William son of my bro. Nathaniel. Exrs. Nathaniel Burwell of Carters Grove, Francis Willis of Gloucester, and sons William and Thomas Nelson. Wit. John Minor, Jr., Edmund Berkeley, Jr., Nelson Berkeley, Jr.

NEW, DANIEL, Gloucester Co., 10 Nov., 1775; 2 May, 1776. Sons Daniel and John; daus. Sarah, Martha Guthrie and Eliz. Garland. Wit. William Duval.

NUTTALL, IRESON, Ware Par., Gloucester Co., 30 Jan., 1797; 3 Feb., 1799. Wife Mary; sister Sarah Hewitt; brothers Henry, Hazlon and Bartlott; sister Nancy Washington Nuttall. Exrs. Mordecai Cooke, Sr., Thomas Cooke, George Booth. Wit. Philip Sansom, Henry L. Nuttall, Mary A. Coleman.

NUTT, MOSELEY, Northumberland Co., 1 March, 1801; 14 April, 1801. Sons William and Walter; dau. Judith Chilton. Exrs. brother Richard Nutt, Wm. Yerby, Geo. Barrett. Wit. Richard Hudnall, Jesse Dawkins, George Pitman.

NEVIL, JAMES, St. Ann's Par., Albemarle Co., 7 March, 1752; 9 Nov., 1752. Son James; son Cornelius Thomas the son of Lucy Nevil; dau. Beth. Allen; dau. Joanna Brown her son John and her eldest dau.; dau. Hannah Matthews; dau.

WILLIAMSBURG WILLS

Mary Douglas; dau. Martha Nevil; dau. Elizabeth Nevil; dau. Judith Nevil; dau. Sally Nevil; my wife. Exrs. George Carrington and Abraham Childers. Wit. John McGourk, John Henderson, Richd. Field, John Griffin, Howell Lewis.

NELSON, WILLIAM, JR., Town and Co. of York, 27 April, 1799; 19 Dec., 1803. Wife Sarah Burwell Nelson; dau. Eliz. Page Harrison Nelson; grandfather William Langston of Co. of Rappahannock; my children. Exrs. brothers Thomas and Philip Nelson. Codicils, dated 20 Oct., 1799, and 22 Oct., 1800.

NORFLEET, CORDALL, Southampton Co., 21 March, 1788; 11 Dec., 1788. Cordall N. Bayrum; daus. Elizabeth and Sarah; son John. Exrs. wife Mary and John and James Wilkinson. Wit. Moses Johnson, John Willeford, James Wilkinson.

NELSON, HUGH, York Co., 18 March, 1790; 20 Jan., 1800. Estate to wife Judith and my children. Exrs. wife and friends Robert Page of Frederick, Hugh Nelson, Jr., of Yorktown and Micajah Crew of Hanover.

OPIE, LINDSY, Northumberland Co., 12 Jan., 1785; 15 March, 1785. Son Thomas to renounce his right of lands that he claims under the will of the late Mr. Wm. Lancaster after the death of his son Joseph Lancaster; son Hierome Lindsy Opie; dau. Sarah Opie; son Leroy Opie; daus. Elizabeth, Susannah, Ann and Janette McAdam Opie. Exrs. Peter Cox, Hudson Muse, Wm. Harding. Wit. Richard Bruer, James Butler, Henry Self, Mary Hall.

OPIE, THOMAS, Northumberland Co., 10 July, 1798; 10 Dec., 1798. Brother Hierome Lindsey Opie; sister Sally Parker; sister Susanna Opie; brother Leroy Opie; sister Jane Opie. Exrs. brother Hierome, Major Thomas Parker, Capt. Wm. Claughton.

PARKER, JOSIAH, Isle of Wight Co., 8 March, 1810; 2
April, 1810. Daughter A. P. P. Cowper; grandson Josiah
Cowper to take the surname of Parker. Exr. son-in-law
Joseph Baker of Nansemond. Wit. Thomas Peirce, Richard
H. Baker, Joseph Pitts, J. B. Southall.

PARKER, PATRICK, Norfolk Co., 29 Aug., 1795. Wife
Mary. Exr. James Hunter partner of Ellison & Hunter of
Norfolk. Wit. Jeremiah Bennett, Samuel Clapp, Mathew
Hawes.

PALMER, JOSEPH, Richmond Co., 31 March, 1749; 7
May, 1750. Wife Ann; son Rawleigh and the balance of estate to be divided between all my children. Exrs. wife and
John Woodbridge. Wit. Charnock Hightour, James Forres-
ter.

PURDIE, GEORGE, Town of Smithfield, Isle of Wight
Co., 11 Nov., 1803; 5 Dec., 1803. Sons Thomas, George and
John; dau. Mary Robinson Diggs; son-in-law Cole Diggs;
friend Mary Ann Hilton. Exrs. wife and three sons. Wit.
Nathaniel Young, Bartholomew Lightfoot.

PURDIE, MARY, Town of Smithfield, Isle of Wight Co.,
3 June, 1809; 4 Dec., 1809. Sons George, John and Thomas;
dau. Mary Robinson wife of Cole Diggs; friend Mary Ann
Hilton. Exrs. my three sons above named. Wit. James Chal-
mers, Joseph Atkinson, Wilson Davis.

PERSON, PHILIP, St. Luke's Par., Southampton Co., 25
Aug., 1781; 9 May, 1782. Brother Turner Person; son Tim-
othy; wife Temperance; dau. Patsy. Exrs. wife and Wm.
Andrews. Wit. Thomas Turner, Richard Clifton, John West-
brook.

PEACHY, THOMAS GRIFFIN, City of Williamsburg, 28
Nov., 1802. Dau.-in-law Mary Monro Peachy wife of my
decd. son Wm. Samuel; my granddaughters; Mr. Cary

WILLIAMSBURG WILLS

grandfather of my little girls; my late wife Eliz. Peachy; my grandsons; granddau. Mary Cary Tabb. Codicil, June, 1807.

PRESSON, WILLIAM, York Co., 7 Jan., 1817; 17 Feb., 1817. Nephew Robert Presson; nephew Callowhill Presson; sister Elizabeth Freeman; friend George Purdie; friend Charles M. Collier; Robert Meek; nephew John Presson. Exrs. George Purdie, Charles M. Collier, Lewis S. Charles. Wit. John C. Robertson, Geo. C. McIntire, Thomas Hunsford.

PRESSON, THOMAS, Warwick Co., 15 April, 1814. Rebecca Crandol; Nancy Ridley; Thomas son of Peter Ridley; John Moore; Molly widow of John Jones; William son of Thomas Jones decd. Exr. Samuel McIntosh. Wit. Samuel McIntosh, Thomas Allen, Samuel M. Allen.

POWELL, LUCY, Par. and Co. of Warwick, 18 Oct., 1813; 10 March, 1814. Cousin Ann Runels; Eliza Ann Custis dau. of Thomas Custis, Jr., and Eliz. his wife. Exr. Thomas Custis. Wit. John Randle, Robert Harrison, William Harrison.

PITT, ROBERT, Accomack Co., 16 Oct., 1755; 30 Nov., 1756. Wife Anne; sons John, Robert and Jabis; dau. Anne; Slocomb Blake; John Blake; brother Jabis Pitts two daughters Elizabeth and Susannah; Thomas Wilkinson; cousin Dennis Blake and Frances his wife. Exrs. wife Anne and friend George Douglas, and sister-in-law Eliz. Rogers. Wit. John Cain, Dennis Blake, Jabis Blake.

PAGE, JOHN, Buck Roe, Elizabeth City Co., 1 May, 1800; 26 June, 1800. Brother Wm. Byrd Page in Fairfax; Dr. Wilson Cary Selden; wife Eliz. King Page; sister Mary Mason Page; Edward, Mary and Thomas Swann; my reputed son John Page Barron of Hampton. Wit. Charles King Mallory, Charles King, John Smith, George Wray.

45

WILLIAMSBURG WILLS

Indenture, dated 15 April, 1795, between John Page of Elizabeth City Co., and Miles King of same place for a marriage between said John Page and Elizabeth King Mallory, dau. of Col. Francis Mallory, decd.

PHILLIPS, WILLIAM, York Co., 25 Jan., 1785; 19 Sept., 1785. Mother Elizabeth Phillips; children of my sister Mary Robinson; sister Nancy Daniel; sister Elizabeth Phillips. Exrs. my mother, Harwood Burt, Thomas Smith. Wit. Thomas Wild, Bernard Elliott, Wm. Throckmorton.

PINCKARD, THOMAS, Lancaster Co., 19 March, 1794; 21 Dec., 1795. Son Thomas; dau. Alice Griffin Pinckard. Exrs. Col. Thomas Gaskins, Wm. Eustace, Charles Leland, Henry Lee Gaskins.

PINCKARD, THOMAS, Lancaster Co., 3 Feb., 1779; 19 Sept., 1782. Wife Frances; grandson Thomas Pinckard; Armistead Currie; Frances Hill Currie and Ellyson Currie all children of my friend David Currie and Elizabeth his wife; George son of Kendall Lee of Northumberland Co.; Kendall Lee son of Capt. Charles Lee of Northumberland Co.; Miss Jane Swann; Samuel Smith McCroskey. Exrs. wife, Charles Carter of Corotoman, Rev. David Currie, Rev. Saml. Smith McCroskey, John Hill Carter, Charles Carter, Wm. Lee, Ellyson Armistead and grandson Thos. Pinckard. Wit. Saml. S. McCroskey, Jane Swann, Christ. Miller, Ellyson Armistead.

PEACHEY, WILLIAM, Essex Co., 21 Jan., 1803; 21 Feb., 1803. Wm. Fleet and James Pendleton; sister Jane Armistead and her dau.; my sister Winifred Trebu; sister Eliz. Pendleton; sister Catherine Ryland; Major Thomas Armistead husband of my sister Jane. Exrs. Wm. Fleet, James Pendleton. Wit. James Jones, Richard Phillips, John Smith, Thomas Boughton.

PAYNE, JESSE, Goochland Co., 6 Oct., 1770; 15 April, 1771. Son George Morton Payne; son Richard Baylor Payne;

WILLIAMSBURG WILLS

wife Frances. Brother George Payne and George Meriwethei guardians and exrs. Wit. Joseph Robinson, Jonathan Fennall, John Pollard, Jr.

PERSON, JOHN, Southampton Co., 10 Feb., 1767; 9 April, 1767. Wife Dorcas; sons Presley, Philip, Colin and Turner. Exrs. wife, brother William Person and cousin Benj. Person. Wit. Allen Jones, Willie Jones, Edward Haynes.

PIGGOTT, PEARSON, James City Co., 5 June, 1787; 13 Aug., 1787. Wife Lucy; son Wm. T. Piggott. Exr. John Brown. Wit. Lewis Bingley, Wm. Piggott, John Piggott.

PARISH, JOHN, Elizabeth City Co., 26 May, 1803; 24 June, 1803. Wife Susannah; son David; two youngest children Susannah and Barbara; my children Frances Cooper, Kitty Banks, Elizabeth Latimer and Nathl. Parishes children and their mother Betsey Parish. Exr. son David. Wit. Charles Jennings, Wm. Parish, Anthony B. Dossemz.

PARISH, DAVID, Elizabeth City Co., 22 Nov., 1805. Wife Rebecca. Exrs. wife and John Skinner, Snr. Wit. Thomas W. Bullock, Wm. H. Skinner, John Skinner.

QUEEN, JOHN, Par. of Suffolk, Nansemond Co., 19 June, 1769; 14 Aug., 1769. Wife Mary and the child she is now supposed to be pregnant with; Priscilla dau. of Abraham and Isabel Avis; James Edwards; William Shepherd Roberts, son of Wm. Shepherd and Lydia Roberts; Levi Solomon and Moses Murphee sons of my bro. Daniel Murphee. Exrs. Wm. Shepherd and Solomon Shepherd, Jr. Wit. John Agnew, Thomas Shepherd, Jesse Fulghan.

ROBINS, WILLIAM, Ware Par., Gloucester Co., 13 July, 1782; 6 July, 1786. Sons John, Thomas and William; son-in-law Isaac Singleton; dau. Rebecca Singleton; grandchildren William, Isaac, Joshua, Thomas, Eliz. and Jane Singleton; children of my son William, viz.: William, Elizabeth, Anne, Susanna and Rebecca Robins; grandchildren Thomas, William, Samuel, James, John and Elizabeth Stubbs; five younger children of John Stubbs; dau. Jane Amory; granddaughter Jane Amory; granddaughter Frances Robins dau. of son John Robins. Exrs. sons John and William Robins, sons-in-law Thomas Chamberlain Amory and Isaac Singleton. Wit. Thomas Acra, Henry Shackelford, William Dudley, Susanna Shackelford, Mary Acra.

ROW, THOMAS, King and Queen Co., 18 Oct., 1789; 14 Dec., 1789. Son Clack Row; child my wife now goes with; son Thomas Gardner Row land adjoining Capt. John Hoskins; son James Row; dau. Anne Row; son Francis Row; daus. Sarah and Elizabeth Gardner Row. Exrs. Capt. William Fleet, Saml. H. Henry. Wit. Anthony Gardner, Wm. Hare, Parmenas Bird, Thomas Evans. Codicil, 27 Oct., 1789, witnessed by Wm. Hare and Eliz. Fleet.

ROBINS, JOSHUA, Northampton Co., 13 Oct., 1786; 10 Feb., 1789. Sons Arthur and William; three eldest daus. Rosey, Sally and Betsy Robins; little son Charles; wife Sarah. Exr. Coventon Simkins. Wit. John Stringer, Snr., John Nathaniel Harden, Margt. Simkins.

REID, JAMES, Town of Urbana, Middlesex Co.. 1 Aug., 1763; 3 Jan., 1764. To be buried in town of Urbana near my brother Adam; to David Ker, Att'y-at-Law; sister Mrs. Jean Reid of Shire of Ayr in Scotland; Sarah wife of John Daniel; John Adair son of Rose O'Neal; godson William son of Major John Robinson; legacy to parish of Christ Church this county. Exrs. Hon. Richard Corbin, Christopher Robinson, David Ker. Wit. John Seymour, James Robb, Archibald Pattison. Codicil, 13 Sept., 1763, witnessed by James Mills and Chas. Neilson.

RAMSAY, JOHN, Borough and Co. of Norfolk, 13 June, 1780; 13 July, 1780. Wife Mary; five daus. Helen, Mary,

WILLIAMSBURG WILLS

Sally, Amy and Fanny Ramsay; nephew James son of brother James Ramsay decd. Exrs. wife, Dr. James Taylor, Dr. Wm. Foshee, Wm. Wishart.

RADWELL, THOMAS, Nansemond Co., 2 Jan., 1819; 12 Sept., 1825. Wife Mary; to Mary K. Fulgham; to Thomas son of Samuel Powell and Sarah dau. of Samuel Powell of Norfolk; to living children of William and Matthew Hays of Knotts Neck. Exrs. Wm. Jordan Sr., Thomas Benn. Wit. George Benn, Charles Thomas, James Arthur.

RESPESS, HENRY, Mathews Co., 12 April, 1807; 14 Dec., 1807. Wife Frances S.; two daus. Lucy Ann and Mary; to children of decd. bro. Richard Respess, viz.; Nancy and Elizabeth; children of decd. bro. Matthew; children of decd. bro. John. Exrs. wife and John D. Jarvis. Wit. Francis Litchfield, John B. Roberts, John D. Jarvis, Eliz. Billups, Joice Billups.

ROUNDTREE, WILLIAM, Par. of Newport, Isle of Wight Co., 5 July, 1796. To Sally Gerner and her dau. Nancy Gerner. Wit. James Martin, John Walker, Mary Parsley.

ROW, CLACK, Caroline Co., 7 Dec., 1803; 14 Feb., 1804. Wife Sarah H. Row and all my children. Exrs. wife, Robert Tunstall, James Jones. Wit. Thomas Magruder, Robert Royston, Wm. Stem.

ROSS, DAVID, St. Peters Par., New Kent. Co., 12 July, 1792; 8 June, 1797. Niece Elizabeth Andrews; nephew John Ross, niece Mary Pond; sister Agnes Furbush; niece Frances Austin; niece Mary Austin; nephew William Ross. Exrs. Armistead Russell, James Power. Wit. A. Russell, James Power.

RIDLEY, MATTHEW, Par. of St. Luke's, Southampton Co., 13 April, 1795; 11 June, 1795. Mother Sarah Drew; Henry son of John Blunt, Sr.; Francis son of Thomas Ridley, Sr.; Thomas son of John Holladay decd. Exrs. uncle Thomas Ridley and Henry Blunt. Wit. Thomas Ridley, Stephen Blake, Amy Ridley, Nancy Blake.

ROBINSON, MARY, Gloucester Co., 10 March, 1803; 4 July, 1803. Niece Frances Yates Robinson dau. of my bro. John Robinson; children of my late sister Whiting. Exrs. nephew Matt. Whiting and Major James Ross of Middlesex. Wit. Giles Cook, W. Taliaferro.

ROBINSON, JOHN, Par. of Christ Church, Middlesex Co., 21 Feb., 1785; 23 July, 1787. Three daus. Judith, Mary and Priscilla Robinson; sons William, John and Christopher; dau. Katherine Robinson; sons Robert and Peter; dau. Eliz. Whiting; nephew Benj. Robinson; Mary Robinson Whiting eldest dau. of Matt. and my dau. Elizabeth Whiting; Eliz. dau. of my nephew Benj. Robinson. Exrs. Philip L. Grymes, nephew Benj. Robinson, sons Christopher and William, and daus. Judith and Mary. Wit. Wm. Stiff, Simon Laighton, Thomas Edwards. Codicil, 28 Jan., 1786, witnessed by Wm. Stiff, John Rootes, Thos. Stiff.

RUFFIN, JOHN, Mecklenburg Co., 10 Aug., 1774; 14 Aug., 1775. Sons Robert, William, John, Thomas and Francis; my wife; daus. Ann, Elizabeth and Martha. Exrs. sons Thomas and Francis. Wit. Henry Delany, Stephen Edward Brodnax.

RUFFIN, ROBERT, King William Co., 10 Jan., 1777. Daughter Martha; sons James, William and Sterling; to Roger Gregory and his sons Richard, Roger, Nathaniel, Thomas and William land in Mecklenburg Co., my daughters. Exrs. wife, son-in-law Herbert Claiborne and my brother John Ruffin. Wit. G. Swinton, Thomas Avery, Reuben Avery, James Clack.

RUSSELL, WILLIAM, Princess Anne Co., 14 Jan., 1790. Nephew Nathan Boys; brother James Russell. Exrs. Peter Evans and Nathan Boys. Wit. Edwd. Valentine, W. Bishop, Wm. Forrest.

WILLIAMSBURG WILLS

RUFFIN, WILLIAM, Surry Co., 15 June, 1809; 25 July, 1809. Brother Francis land in this county; my mama to have use of my negroes during her life; to children of Reuben Butler and Thomas Edwards; to Mary Lee Harris; sister Susan Ruffin. Exr. brother Francis. Wit. Charles H. Graves.

RUFFIN, WILLIAM, Surry Co., 1 May, 1773; 26 April, 1774. Wife Lucy; dau. Elizabeth; dau. ———; my youngest son———; son Theodorick Bland Ruffin; mentions his father-in-law Col. Theodorick Bland; bro. John Ruffin to be guardian to my son Theodorick; bro. Thomas Ruffin; Wm. Browne, Richard Taliaferro, Jr., John Hartwell Cocke. Exrs. Thomas and John Ruffin, Jr. Wit. Nicholas ———, Jr., Edmund Ruffin, Jr., Edward Archer, Wm. Ward, Lewis Williams, Edmund Waller.

RANSDELL, EDWARD, Cople Par., Westmoreland Co., 19 June, 1773; 30 Nov., 1773. Wife Elizabeth; dau. Elizabeth and her husband James Davenport; brothers Wharton and William Ransdell; Richard Parker; nephew Ransdell son of Joseph Peirce; nephew Cresly son of my bro. Wharton Ransdell; Edward son of my bro. William. Extx. wife. Wit. Mary Purcell, Thomas Thompson, Richard Parker.

ROBINSON, JUDITH, Par. Christ Church, Middlesex Co., 8 May, 1803; 24 Feb., 1806. Brother Peter Robinson; Judith dau. of bro. Robert Robinson. Exr. bro. William Robinson.

ROBINSON, WILLIAM, Middlesex Co., 11 Nov., 1807; 28 Dec., 1807. Wife Elizabeth; dau. Lucy Lilly. Exrs. wife and Carter B. Berkeley. Wit. Lucy B. Churchill, Needler Robinson, Henry Heffernan, Wm. Wake, Tom Stiff.

ROBINSON, NEEDLER, New Kent Co., 19 Dec., 1822; 8 Jan., 1823. Nephew Wm. Robinson of Benville, King and Queen Co.; niece Alice C. Jennings and her children, viz.; Robert C., Robinsonova, Needler R., Indiana, James Roddy,

Alice Octavia; five children of my nephew William Robinson, viz.: Ann, Gabriella, Martha, Benjamin and William; three children of my decd. niece Eliza. C. Piemont, viz.: Eliz. H. C., Amanda N., and Robinson. Wit. Patrick Gannon, Jesse Cogbies.

SHERMAN, WILLIAM, New Kent Co., 24 May, 1796; 8 Dec., 1796. Wife Rebecca; sons Ballard, William and Thomas; daus. Rebecca, Milly, Elizabeth Carter and Nancy Ammons; grandsons Abner and Wm. Clopton; son-in-law William Ammons. Codicil, 24 Sept., 1796, grandson Wm. Moss Sherman, and the child that the widow of my son William now goes with. Wit. C. Christian, A. Christian.

SHERMAN, THOMAS, New Kent Co., 18 July, 1801; 10 Dec., 1801. Nephew Wm. Moss Sherman; nephew Abner Clopton; sister Mildred Courtnay; nephew Thomas Ballard Sherman; nephew Ballard Ammons. Exrs. nephew Wm. Sherman, brother Ballard Sherman and Francis Oley. Wit. Nathl. Cowles, C. C. C., James Oley, Antheline Gay, Wm. Crump.

SHACKLEFORD, LYNE, of Curls, Henrico Co., 10 May, 1806; 6 Oct., 1806. Wife Eliza Price; daus. Betsy, Patsy and Nancy; son George; dau. Mary. Exrs. James Spark of Mathews and Wm. Chamberlayne of New Kent. Wit. William Dandridge, James Vaughan.

SCROSBY, JOHN, Gloucester Co., no date; 8 Feb., 1791. Brother James, nephew John Cooke son of Mordecai and Eliz. Cooke; niece Nanny Timson Buckner two hundred and fifty pounds when she arrives at lawful age or marries. Exrs. brother-in-law Mordecai Cooke, Richard Baynham. Wit. Thomas Stiff, William Stiff.

SPADY, MASSY, Town of Portsmouth, Norfolk Co., 25 Feb., 1826; 18 Sept., 1826. Daughter Abigail Bradshaw; Jesse Spady decd.; grandsons Thomas and John Bradshaw;

grandchildren John, Elizabeth, Sarah and Samuel Darling. Wit. James P. Peed, Samuel Hain, Ebenezer Thompson.

SPRATT, DANIEL, Town of Urbana, Middlesex Co., no date; 28 Dec., 1807. Aunt Mrs. Frances Daniel; Genl. John Minor and John Chew; my relative Robert Beverley Fife, near Edinburgh, Scotland; James Fife of same place; William Fife of same place; aunt Mrs. Catherine Fife of same place; Margaret Spratt dau. of Margt. Law of Fifeshire, Scotland; Charles son of Genl. John Minor; Dr. James Dabney of Gloucester. Exrs. John Minor and John Chew. Wit. Samuel W. Sayre, David C. Ker, George French.

SPRATT, ROBERT BEVERLEY, Urbana, Middlesex Co., 18 Feb., 1805; 22 April, 1805. Brother George Daniel Spratt; children of my half sister Charlotte Gwathney; Robert Beverley Fife near Edinburgh, the said Robert B. Fife is a son of Catherine Fife, sister of my father the late Dr. Robert Spratt; Frances widow of Col. George Daniel. Exrs. brother George D. Spratt, Col. Thomas Roane, James Ross, Staige Davis. Wit. John Chew, Jr., Peter Kemp, Jr., Wm. Simcoe, Jr.

SPRAGGIN, REBECCA, James City, 8 May, 1803; 11 June, 1804. Sister Judith Harwood; nephew Washington Cowles. Exr. Wm. Brown, Snr. Wit. Wm. Brown, Jr., John E. Brown, John Cowles.

STARKE, PHILEMON,, King and Queen Co., 13 Aug., 1753; 10 March, 1756. Ann Mackendree; late brother Flurry Starke. Extx. Ann Mackendree. Wit. Joseph Orrill, Elizabeth Orrill.

STARKE, FLURRY, St. Stephens Par., King and Queen Co., 22 March, 1753; 12 June, 1753. Wife Ann; Jane dau. of Henry Coleman; Sally dau. of John Phelps, bros. William and Philemon Starke. Exrs. wife and bro. William. Wit. Henry Coleman, Joseph Ferguson, John Phelps.

WILLIAMSBURG WILLS

SEWARD, WM. CAUFELL, Par. of Southwark, Surry Co., 5 Nov., 1780; 26 March, 1782. Children Caufell and Martha; aunt Elizabeth Hamlin; sister Polly Harris; brother Edward Seward. Exrs. Nicholas and Jacob Faulcon. Wit. Michael Blow, Joel Wall, H. Blunt.

SAUNDERS, ALEXANDER, So. Farnham Par., Essex Co., 26 Nov., 1777; 18 May, 1778. Wife Mary; sons William; Alexander, Edward and Henry; daus. Susanna and Fanny. Exrs. wife, son William and Capt. Wm. Gatewood. Wit. W. Young, Sallea Hunleay, Wm. Brooke.

SUMMERELL, HENRY, Southampton Co., 4 Oct., 1801. Wife Diannah and the child she now goes with; son Josiah H., dau. Rebecca. Exrs. wife, Wm. Holden, Silas Summerell. Wit. John Boresten, Benj. Holden, John Warren.

STONE, MARY, widow of Simon, Princess Anne Co., 25 March, 1817; 7 June, 1819. Eldest son Daniel; son Thomas; decd. father John Henley, Snr., dau. Fanny Overstreet. Exr. son Daniel Stone. Wit. Ann Ewell, Anna Henley, Fanny Benthall, Lydia Benthall.

SMITH, MARY, City of Williamsburg, 15 Dec., 1813; 26 Feb., 1816. Nelly, Eve and Sally Bolling; Benj. White; Beverley Rowsey; Rachel White and her sister Fanny; Mary wife of David Meade Randolph; Mrs. Tucker wife of St. George Tucker; Robert Greenhow ; Sally Anderson; Rev John Bracken; Sally and Rachel Anderson; William White; relation Jennie Westwood dau. of William Westwood decd. of Hampton. Exr. Robert Anderson. Wit. George Jackson, William Browne.

STITH, GRIFFIN, Northampton Co., 9 June, 1794; 9 Sept. 1799. Dr. James Lyon, Nathaniel Goffigon and John Eyre to sell my land and divide the proceeds between my wife and children. Exr. Nathl. Goffigon.

WILLIAMSBURG WILLS

SALLARD, SIMON, Par. of Lunenburg, Richmond Co., 23 Nov., 1769; 5 March, 1770. Mother Blanche Sallard; decd. father Simon Sallard; wife Eliza; son Simon; dau. Jane Sallard; brother John. Exrs. wife, Avery Dyes, Thomas Hibert. Wit. Geo. H. Fauntleroy, William Buckland, John Walker.

STIFF, THOMAS, Par. of Christ Church, Middlesex Co., 3 Aug., 1816. Wife Elizabeth; daus. Mary C., Eliz. D., and Louisa S. M.; the children of James Stiff. Exrs. wife, Carter B. Berkeley, Dr. Geo. M. McIntire.

SUTTON, ROWLAND, Middlesex Co., 6 March, 1782; 28 Oct., 1782. Son John Gayle Sutton; daus. Mary Diggs and Nancy Dudley. Exrs. wife, William Diggs, Charles Dudley. Wit. George Bush, David Powell.

SCROSBY, JAMES, Par. of Christ Church, Middlesex Co., no date; 23 March, 1772. Wife Ann; sons John, James and Robert; daughters Elizabeth and Dorothy; brother Charles Lee. Exrs. Robert Mathews, Wm. Stiff. Wit. William Stiff, Mary Wake.

SCROSBY, JAMES, Mathews Co., 9 Feb., 1792; April Court, 1792. Nephew John Cooke; nephews Mordecai, Thomas and Buckner sons of Mordecai Cooke; friends Dr. Wm. Baynham and Richard Baynham; niece Ann T. Buckner one negro woman after my mother's death, and given to me by my uncle Richard Mathews; my sister Dorothy Buckner; John Mathews of Essex. Exrs. Richard Baynham, Mordecai Cooke. Wit. A. Flippen, John Humphries.

STEPTOE, ELIZABETH, Westmoreland Co., 1 Sept., 1801; 26 Oct., 1802. Keziah Pendegrass; to Mrs. Sally Newton; to Mrs. Alice Jones and Mrs. Mary Parker; Ransdell Pierce; brother-in-law James Steptoe; Henry Neale son of Penelope Moxley; Margaret Wilkinson; Elijah Ransdell of Kentucky; John Wickham of city of Richmond; Elder Henry

WILLIAMSBURG WILLS

Toler and Elder Andrew Broadaz; mentions late son Edward Steptoe whose remains lie in George Town, Maryland, aged 13 years and 3 months. Exr. Mr. Samuel Templeman. Codicils, 16 April, 1802, and 13 Feb., 1802. Wit. Sally Newton, Angelica Collins, Willoughby Newton.

SMITH, THOMAS, Isle of Wight, 17 April, 1799; 2 Sept., 1799. Five daughters Elizabeth Johnston, Sarah, Fanny, Jenny and Lillias Smith; wife Eliza; son Arthur to be educated to be a physician. Exrs. wife, and son-in-law Major James Johnston. Wit. James Young, David Dick, Edward Burt.

STUBBLEFIELD, MARY, Gloucester Co., 24 Sept., 1823; 3 Nov., 1823. Cary Hall; William Leavitt; Richard Jones; niece Mary Ann Sturges. Wit. John Nicholson, John Coffee.

STUBBLEFIELD, THOMAS, Ware Parish, Gloucester Co., 3 Feb., 1805; 1 Dec., 1823. Wife Mary; sons Baylor F., and Thomas M. Stubblefield; daus. Mary and Sally. Exrs. brother Simon Stubblefield, John S. Scott. Wit. Robert Stubblefield, Nathaniel Wilkins.

SMITH, ROBERT, Town and Co. of York, mariner, 1 Feb., 1813; 16 May, 1814. Uncle Robert Gibbons sole legatee and exr. Wit. Corbin Griffin, John Grant, N. Taylor.

SMITH, LAWRENCE, Par. of York Hampton, York Co., 2 Nov., 1778; 15 Feb., 1779. Wife Damaris; my son and my three daughters. Wit. Philip Dedman, John Gibbons, Snr., Aug. Moore.

SMITH, THOMAS, Rector of Cople, Westmoreland Co., 10 Dec., 1788; 27 Oct., 1789. Sons Thomas Gregory and John Augustine; wife Mary; daus. Sarah and Mary; godson Baldwin Mathews. Exrs. wife, brother Col. Gregory Smith, Philip Lee. Wit. Mary Smith, Elizabeth Buckner, Richard Buckner, Henry Tapscott, Martin Tapscott.

WILLIAMSBURG WILLS

TALIAFERRO, RICHARD, James City., 3 Feb., 1775; 9 Aug., 1779. Land and houses in city of Williamsburg to dau. Elizabeth and her husband Mr. George Wythe; grandson Richard Taliaferro; my other grandchildren. Exrs. son Richard and son-in-law George Wythe. Wit. Gabriel Maupin. Benj. Waller, Benj. C. Waller.

TOMKIES, CHARLES, physician, Gloucester Co., no date; 27 Oct., 1737. Three daughters Elizabeth, Mary and Catherine; sons Charles and Francis; wife Mary extx.; Thomas Edwards and son Francis trustees. Wit. John Edwards, David Alexander, Thomas Baytop.

TENNISS, AARON, York Co., 3 July, 1813; 10 Oct., 1813. Willis Wilson; nephew Josiah and niece Harriet Shelton; brother John Tenniss; brother Abraham Tenniss; dau. Elizabeth Grey; brothers Richard, John and Jesse Tenniss; sister Mary Lewis; my mother. Exrs. James Shelton, Henry Grey, Willis Wilson. Wit. Saml. Colton,, Smith Bunting, John S. Westwood, Wm. S. Sclater.

THOROWGOOD, JOHN WILLIAM, Princess Anne Co., 1 Oct., 1804; 3 Dec., 1804. Wife Frances and her father Wm. Thorowgood; godson Billy son of Enoch Jones; niece Mrs. Sukey Williams Singleton; goddaughter Nancy dau. of Henry Cornick; Miss Margt. Jamison; Mr. James Kempe; nephews James and John Thorogood. Exrs. wife and James Haynes of the Western Shore. Wit. Thos. Ryan Butler, Wm. W. Michael, John W. Broughton.

TURNER, WILLIAM, James City Co., 17 Nov., 1809; 11 Dec., 1809. Friend Wm. P. Harris; my father John Turner and my brothers and sisters by my mother Mary Turner. Extr. my father. Wit. Wm. Allen, A. D. Galt, Richard Shackelford.

TUCKER, ROBERT, JR., Norfolk Co., 9 July, 1779; no date of probate. Brother-in-law Thomas Newton, Jr.; my three unmarried sisters Molly, Nanny and Caroline Henrietta Tucker; mother Joanna Tucker; brother Corbin; sisters Sarah Taylor and Frances Hervey. Exrs. Thomas Newton, Jr., Preeson Bowdoin, Genl. Thomas Nelson. Codicil, dated 19 Sept., 1779, mentions sister Joanna Corbin; nephew James Taylor; nephew Thomas son of Thomas Newton, Jr.; sister Courtney; nephew Richard Corbin; niece Betsy Taylor Corbin; nieces Nancy, Felicia and Jane Corbin; nieces Amy and Sarah Newton; niece Elizabeth dau. of Joseph Hutchings; niece Sarah dau. of John Taylor; friend Robert Brit. Same exrs. as above. Wit. Wm. Smith, Sarah Smith, John Freeman.

TAYLOR, RICHARD, Prince George Co., 13 Nov., 1799; — June, 1801. Wife Mary plantation in Nottoway; son Richard Field Taylor; daus. Nanny Birchell, Eliz. and Sally Taylor; granddaughters Martha Douglas Holloway and Mary Taylor Holloway daus. of my late dau. Mary Holloway. Wit. Wm. Twitty, B. Puryear, Edmund Birckett.

TRAVIS, SAMUEL, City of Williamsburg, 1 July, 1821; 23 July, 1821. Mentions land in Kentucky left by his father; brother Robert B. Travis; wife Eliz. R. Travis and my children. Exrs. brother Robert and brother-in-law Jesse Cole. Wit. A. D. Galt, John C. Pryor, Wm. Pearman.

TUCKER, ROBERT, Borough of Norfolk, 10 Jan., 1765; 4 Aug., 1769. Sons Robert and Gawin Corbin Tucker; my uncle John Tucker whose heir-at-law I am; daus. Sarah, Martha, Courtney, Ann and Frances; wife Joanna; dau. Mary; dau. Joanna wife of Gawin Corbin, Esq.; wife, Honl. Richard Corbin and brother John Tucker guardians of my children. Exrs. wife, Richard Corbin, John Tucker, Wm. Nelson, John Taylor. Wit. John Lee, John Thompson, Wm. Michel. Codicil, dated 12 Jan., 1765. Same witnesses.

THOROWGOOD, JOHN, Princess Anne Co., 13 Dec., 1800; 4 April, 1803. Son John Wainhouse Thorowgood; son

WILLIAMSBURG WILLS

Adam; dau. Susannah wife of James Thorowgood, their son John and the child my dau. is now pregnant with; grandson James Thorowgood; nephew James Kempe; granddaughter Susannah Wainhouse Thorowgood. Exrs. brother Mitchell Thorowgood and my sons John W., and Adam Thorowgood. Wit. Thomas Newton, Jr., Peggy Jamison, Henry Mackie.

VAUGHAN, RABLEY, St. Johns Par., King William Co., 4 May, 1787; 25 June, 1787. Brothers Stamp, Rowlin, Henry, James, Edmund and Lewis Vaughan; sisters Molly Christian and Elizabeth Vading and my brother Millin Vaughan's children. Wit. Edward Pye Chamberlayne, John Ware.

VAUGHAN, ROBERT B., York Co., 21 March, 1822; 17 June, 1822. Sister Mary Ann wife of George B. Lightfoot; sister Harriet P. Weathers; sister Eliza T. Weathers; sister Georgiana Weathers; mother Mary Weathers; late father William Vaughan. Wit. A. Marston, W. J. Bowis, John T. Marston.

WEBB, WILLIAM, Northumberland Co., 13 July, 1763; 12 Sept., 1763. Son John Webb, Jr.; son William lands adjoining John Webb; sons Wildey, Motty and George; daus. Elizabeth, Charity and Milly. Exrs. John Edmunds, John Rogers. Wit. Elizabeth Cottrell, Elizabeth Shepherd.

WASHINGTON, AUGUSTINE, George Town, Dist. of Columbia, 12 July, 1810; 8 Oct., 1810. Son Bushrod land in Westmoreland Co. purchased of Henry Washington; son George Corbin Washington land purchased of John Hood Washington called Indiantown; my son's uncle the late General George Washington; my decd. dau. Ann Robinson; wife Sarah; dau. Sarah Tayloe; my wife to be guardian to dau. Sarah and son Wm. Augustine. Exrs. wife, son George Corbin and friend Robert Beverley. Wit. Charlotte Fitzhugh, Charles Worthington, Frances S. Key.

WEST, MARY, Petsworth Parish Gloucester Co., 23 Sept., 1782;4 March, 1784. Daughter Betty Hibble and her dau.

WILLIAMSBURG WILLS

Elizabeth; granddaughter Mary Davis; dau. Nanny Haines; grandson Richard West Haines; dau. Mary Davis. Exr. son-in-law George Hibble. Wit. Thomas Douglas, Elizabeth Davis.

WILKINSON, WILLIAM, Nansemond Co., 29 Sept., 1807; 13 Oct., 1807. Son John; granddaughter Adaline Amelia Wilkinson Godwin the land I obtained in Tennessee by marriage with my last wife; friend John Bristow. Exrs. son John and John Barber.

WILKINSON, MILLS, Nansemond Co., 13 Jan., 1804; 10 April, 1804. Nephew Wm. W. Wright son of Stephen Wright Snr.; nephew Nathaniel Wilkinson and niece Elizabeth Wilkinson; Alexander and Sally children of my brother Willis Wilkinson; William and Lewis children of my brother B. Wilkinson; to Dr. Willis Wilkinson; relative Peter Minton; my sister; relatives Harrison and Mills Minton. Exr. Stephen Wright. Wit. J. Poole, Roland Darden, Wm .Jordan.

WILKINSON, JOHN D., James City Co., 19 March, 1814; 9 May, 1814. Daughter Elizabeth Travis; children of my brother Cary Wilkinson of Charles City Co., and children of my two sisters Polly Poindexter and Judith Crump of New Kent Co.; grandson John D. Travis. Exr. brother Cary Wilkinson. Wit. Wm. E. Barrett, John J. Miles, Wm. Taylor.

WILLS, JOHN, Warwick Co., 19 April, 1800; 8 Sept., 1803. Daughter Elizabeth S.; son John; wife Ann; son Miles C. Exrs. brother Wm. S. Wills and my wife. Wit. W. Dudley, John Jones, Samuel Wills.

WEBB, MOTLEY, Northumberland Co., but now in the service of the U. S., 25 Jan., 1779; 13 June, 1785. Lands on the Potomac river to my brother John and he to be exr. Wit. Elisha Harcum, Wm. Corbell, Jesse Harcum.

WEBB, MATTHIAS, Isle of Wight Co., 23 Jan., 1785; 3 March, 1785. Wife Nancy; children Patsy, Fanny, Betsy and

James Webb. Exrs. wife, brother Samuel Webb and John Jennings Wheadon. Wit. John Davis, John Harrison, Benj, Jones.

WATTS, JANE, Elizabeth City Co., 26 April, 1797; 7 Jan., 1798. My husband Samuel; granddaughter Euphan Russell; dau. Sarah Sandifer; granddaughters Elizabeth and Sarah N. Buxton. Exr. grandson John Cooper. Wit. Samuel Watts, Jr., Ann Sheppard.

WALL, JOEL, Surry Co., 15 May, 1799; 24 Feb., 1801. Son Patrick; wife Rebecca; dau. Polly; the child my wife is now pregnant with. Exrs. wife and Isham Inman. Wit. John Warren, James Judkins, Sr., James Wall.

WALKER, ROBERT, James City Co., 7 Jan., 1804; 25 Nov., 1804. Wife Elizabeth; sons Walter and Wayn; dau. Louisa. Exr. brother William Walker. Wit. Wm. Walker, Jr., John Walker, Edmond Cowles, Sr.

WALKER, EDWARD, Bath Parish, Dinwiddie Co., 9 Aug., 1781; Nov. Court, 1781. Land in Brunswick to sons Nathaniel and John; wife Priscilla. Exrs. Richard Sharpe, brother Robert Walker, Col. Daniel Fisher, John King and John Burwell. Wit. Peter Parish, Jas. Jennings, Benj. Mathews.

WALKER, JOHN, late of Va., but now of Town of Nassau, Island of New Providence, merchant, Bahama Islands; 26 July, 1784; 13 Dec., 1784. Brother William Walker of the Arms Bank, Glasgow, and his children. Exrs. friends Wm. Chisholm, John Ferguson, John Boyd and Dugald Ruthven.

WALKE, WILLIAM, Princess Anne Co., 13 March, 1790; 6 July, 1795. Wife Mary; son Anthony; my children. Exrs. wife, Cornelius Calvert, Jr., Saunders T. Calvert. Wit. Mary Walke, Sr., Frances Walke, Hillary Snale.

WILLIAMSBURG WILLS

WALKE, MARY, relict of William, Princess Ann Co., 9 Oct., 1797; 24 Sept., 1798. Son Anthony; daus. Elizabeth, Mary and Anne; son William; my children's decd. uncles E. H. Walke and J. B. Walke. Exrs. my children.

WHITING, FRANCIS, of Eaton Hill, Gloucester Co., 6 May, 1825; 6 Feb., 1826. To the trustees of Gloucester Charity School one-third of my estate; dau. Ellinor and son John five cents each; son Francis B. Whiting one-third of estate; servant Hannah Graves and her dau. Harriett Fayette Graves.

WESTBROOKE, WILLIAM, Southampton Co., 8 Nov., 1801; — Feb., 1805. To Miles Benberry bastard son of Sally Benberry; Mourning Webb; sisters Rebecca Tillar and Sally Andrews; Nancy dau. of Kirby Bittle; Betsy and Priscilla daus. of aforesaid Kirby; to Lucy Bittle wife of said Kirby; John Henry Persons Westbrooke; brother Henry Westbrooke decd.; Mason Westbrooke (female); brother Thomas Westbrooke and Peggy his wife and their dau. Harriet; Sally Andrews. Exrs. Thomas Westbrooke, John Applewhite, Saml. Blunt. Wit. John Barham, John Magee, Valentine Simmons.

WEST, RALPH, County not stated; ———, 1798. To son Robert land purchased of Priscilla West, 23 Dec., 1793, in Isle of Wight Co.; daus. Hannah, Sally and Peggy West. Exr. brother Thomas King.

WEBB, JAMES, St. Bride's Par., Norfolk Co., 4 July, 1792. No date of probate. Wife Sarah; son James Kader Webb; son John Corprew Webb; daus. Sarah and Penelope. Exrs. wife and Kader Webb. Wit. Nancy Corprew, Fanny Shepherd, Joshua Corprew, George Calles.

WADDEY, EDWARD S., Borough of Norfolk, 7 July, 1815; 18 Jan., 1819. Mentions his co-partnership with John D. Brown under the firm name of Edward S. Waddey & Co.; wife Sarah; decd. brother Daniel R. Waddey; to all my children. Exrs. wife and Edward Frith. Wit. John D. Brown, Ephraim Wheeler, Francis H. Hoyer.

WADDEY, JOHN R., Northampton Co., 1 Oct., 1814; 10 April, 1815. My wife; son Edward R. Waddey; son John R. Waddey; decd. brother Daniel R. Waddey; daus. Mary J., Emeline, Eliza and Mary Jacob Waddey; Dr. Jacob G. Parker to be guardian to my sons; Thomas S. Satchell guardian to my daughters, and the two guardians above named to be exrs.

WODDROP, JOHN, Charles City Co., 7 Dec., 1774; 4 Aug., 1779. Wife Mary; son John land in Nansemond and Isle of Wight; dau. Mary Ann. Exrs. Walter Peter, brother-in-law Samuel Harwood and John Brown. Wit. Wm. Acrill, Wm. Emery, Henry Young.

WODDROP, JOHN, merchant, Nansemond Co., 9 Oct., 1765; 9 June 1766. Wife Ann; sons John and Alexander; daus. Elizabeth, Margaret, Ann and Lilias. Exrs. wife and son John. Wit. Wm. Hamilton, James Hamilton, Anthony Warwick.

WODDROP, ANN., Nansemond Co., 7 Sept., 1785; 8 June, 1789. Son Alexander; grandson John Woddrop; dau. Elizabeth Smith; dau. Margt. Edmonds; dau. Ann Dick; dau. Lilias Woddrop. Exr. son Alexander. Wit. Wm. Baldwin, Joseph Godwin, Cornelius Jones.

WILLOUGHBY, JOHN, Norfolk Co., 28 Feb., 1786; 19 Sept., 1791. Sons Thomas and John L. Willoughby; daus. Ann, Margaret, Lucy, Elizabeth and Martha Willoughby. Exrs. Thomas Ritson, John Leigh. Wit. Francis Leigh, Nanny Leigh.

WILSON, WILLIS, Portsmouth, Norfolk Co., 2 Dec.; 1796; 17 Dec., 1798. Estate to wife Mary. Wit. John Davis, J. Blamire, James S. Mathews, Aaron Milhade.

WILLIAMSBURG WILLS

WILLS, GEORGE G., St. John's Par., King William Co., 26 June, 1785. Wife Betsy; sons William and George G. Wills. Exrs. Wm. Inge, Anderson Claybrook. Wit. Wm. Lipscomb, Hardin Lipscomb, Wm. Trimmer.

WILLS, NATHANIEL, Isle of Wight Co., 25 Oct., 1821; 1 Sept., 1823. Wife Eliza S.; Mary Ann dau. of Parker Wills; Nathaniel son of said Parker Wills; mother Prudence Holladay; Nathaniel Wills Nosworthy; Christopher Reynolds; brother Willis Williams; Mary wife of Joseph Godwin. Exr. Willis Williams. Wit. Wm. Holleman, B. W. Beville.

WOODSIDE, JOHN, Borough of Norfolk, 2 Dec., 1800; 26 Jan., 1801. Son Robert and Elizabeth his wife; granddaughter Jane Woodside; son James; dau. Elizabeth Whitney; granddaughter Jane Whitney; son John; wife Anne; son Robert and son-in-law Michael Curran guardians to son John. Exrs. son Robert and Thomas Newton, Jr. Wit. James Nimmo, Danl. Baxter, Tully R. Wise.

WRIGHT, PATRICK, City of Richmond, 8 Dec., 1786; 1 Jan., 1787. Wife Lucy; brother John Wright; son George; my children. Exrs. Geo. Muter, George Kelly, Richard Evans, Sr. Wit. Charles Hay, John Cunliffe, John McColl.

WILSON, JAMES, St. Brides Par., Norfolk Co., 27 Sept., 1817; 19 Dec., 1820. Sons Nathaniel, Caleb and Tatem Wilson; son William. Exrs. sons James E. Wilson and Caleb Wilson. Wit. John Dorney, John W. Wilson, Frederick Wilkins, Wm. Wilson, Jr.

WILSON, WILLIAM, JR., Par of St. Brides, Norfolk Co., 17 March, 1787; 20 April, 1787. Brother James Wilson; Malachi Wilson, Jr.; brother Tatem Wilson; sister Love Wilson; Bassett Butt, Sr., son of Ann Butt. Exrs. friends James Wilson, Sr., and James Webb., Jr. Wit. Thomas Holstead,

64

Malachi Wilson, Jr., Rasha Butt, John Hodges, Jr., Willis Wilson, Jr.

WILSON, GOODRICH, Portsmouth, Norfolk Co., 16 Nov., 1785; 16 Dec., 1785. Wife Louisa; daus. Nancy, Peggy and Harriet; sons Samuel, Goodrich and George. Exrs. wife and brother Sampson Wilson. Wit. Joseph Gray, Frances Day, Paul Wallington, Betsy Day.

YERBY, GEORGE, North Farnham Par., Richmond Co., 23 May, 1785; 3 June, 1793. Sons John M. and George, land in Lancaster county; daus. Sarah M., Nancy, Judith G., and Betsy Yerby. Exrs. friends Wm. Miskell, John Fauntleroy, Abner Dobyns, Thaddeus Williams. Wit. Chichester Tapscott, Sally Keyser, Ellen Ball Glascock.

INDEX

INDEX

Bishop, 34, 50
Bittle, 62
Blake, 45, 50
Blamire, 63
Bland, 33, 51
Blincoe, 34
Blow, 31, 54
Blunt, 22, 32, 33, 37, 49, 54, 62
Bohannon, 5, 8
Bolling, 54
Booker, 35
Booth, 6, 7, 31, 42
Boresten, 54
Boswell, 6, 20
Boughton, 46
Boush, 8, 9, 18
Boushell, 10
Bowdoin, 58
Bowen, 36
Bowers, 23, 24
Bowis, 59
Bowman, 29
Boyce, 31
Boyd, 7, 9, 13, 34, 61
Boykin, 9, 10
Boys, 50
Brack, 6
Bracken, 15, 29
Bradenham, 10
Bradley, 10, 15, 23
Bradshaw, 52
Bragg, 10
Bramble, 12
Branch, 8, 11
Branghile, 26
Brany, 10
Braxton, 10, 20
Bray, 19
Brewer, 6
Bridger, 7, 8, 31, 36
Briggs, 15, 32, 34
Brisell, 18
Bristow, 60
Brit, 58

Broadaz, 56
Brockenbrough, 14, 17
Brodnax, 50
Bromadges, 10
Brooke, 9, 17, 54
Brooks, 7, 15, 32
Brough, 31
Broughton, 57
Brown, 7, 11, 14, 16, 35, 41, 42, 47, 53, 63
Browne, 11, 19, 51, 54
Bruce, 8
Bruer, 43
Bryan, 20, 23
Buchanan, 39
Buckland, 55
Buckner, 6, 7, 52, 55, 56
Bullifant, 38
Bullock, 47
Bunting, 7, 57
Burbidge, 21
Burges, 40
Burnett, 23
Burt, 7, 46, 56
Burton, 12, 33
Burwell, 7, 10, 20, 27, 42, 61
Bush, 55
Bushnell, 13
Butcher, 41
Butler, 43, 51, 57
Butt, 7, 64
Butts, 15, 16
Buxton, 61
Byan, 35

C.

Cain, 45
Callcote, 29
Calles, 62
Calvert, 13, 17, 61
Cammel, 12
Camp, 14
Campbell, 13, 14, 28
Cargill, 15

INDEX

INDEX

INDEX

Jamison, 57, 59
Jannis, 31
Janson, 40
Jarvis, 33, 49
Jefferson, 8
Jeffries, 34
Jenne, 12
Jennings, 47, 51, 61
Johnson, 12, 23
Johnston, 56
Jones, 10, 13, 14, 20, 21, 25, 27, 32, 33, 34, 35, 36, 45, 46, 47, 49, 55, 56, 57, 60, 61, 63
Jordan, 49, 60
Joyne, 33
Judkins, 61

K.

Keen, 14
Keene, 34
Keingham, 22
Kellor, 27
Kelsick, 34
Kells, 34
Kelly, 14, 28, 33, 64
Kemp, 21, 34, 36, 53, 57, 59
Kennon, 33
Ker, 33, 48, 53
Key, 59
Keyser, 65
King, 32, 34, 45, 46, 61, 62
Klug, 36, 41
Knight, 29

L.

Lacy, 21
Laighton, 50
Lancaster, 43
Landrum, 30
Lane, 16
Langston, 43
Langstone, 35, 39
Lankford, 31, 36
Larke, 15

Lashly, 34, 35
Latane, 17
Latimer, 47
Law, 53
Lawrence, 36
Léavitt, 56
Lee, 14, 17, 21, 32. 34, 46, 55, 56, 58
Leigh, 23, 35, 63
Leipine, 37
Leland, 28, 46
Lemmon, 6
Lester, 15, 35
Lewis, 25, 35, 40, 43, 57
Lightfoot, 6, 35, 41, 44, 59
Lindsay, 13, 32
Lipscomb, 64
Litchfield, 49
Littleton, 38
Lorey, 17
Lorimer, 34
Lorton, 40
Lowe, 8
Lowry, 35
Lucas, 13, 14
Lupo, 39
Lyon, 10, 54

M.

MacKendree, 53
Mackie, 40, 59
Maclean, 17
Macon, 20
Magee, 62
Magruder, 49
Major, 38, 40
Mallory, 7, 39, 45, 46
Manning, 12
March, 39
Marks, 16
Marrable, 38
Marriot, 25
Marston, 38, 41, 59
Martin, 11, 24, 49

INDEX